The Catholic
Case for
Contraception

The Catholic Case for Contraception

Edited by
Daniel Callahan

The Macmillan Company
Collier-Macmillan Limited, London

ACKNOWLEDGMENTS

Grateful acknowledgment is made to the following for permission to reprint articles and excerpts which originally appeared under their imprint:

COMMONWEAL

"Contraception and the Council," March 11, 1966
"The Right to Dissent," Aug. 23, 1968
"The Encyclical Crisis," Sept. 6, 1968

NATIONAL CATHOLIC REPORTER

"Majority and Minority Birth Control Commission Reports," April 19, 1967
"The Encyclical," Aug. 7, 1968
"Theologians' Statement," Aug. 14, 1968

FIDES PUBLISHERS

"Personal Reflections on Birth Control," from *Christian Morality Today* by Charles E. Curran, 1966

SHEED AND WARD

"Procreation and Control," from *Beyond Birth Control: The Christian Experience of Sex* by Sidney Cornelia Callahan, © Sheed and Ward, Inc., 1968

NC NEWS SERVICE

Translation of *Humanae Vitae*

MARRIAGE

"A Biologist Asks Some Questions," June, 1967

Contents

Introduction

The publication on July 29, 1968, of Pope Paul's encyclical *Humanae Vitae,* "Of Human Life," marked the end of one era and the beginning of another. The era the end of which it marked was that of a period of papal indecision on licit methods of birth regulation. This indecision was brought about by almost a decade of intense discussion by a large number of theologians and priests who sought a way of bringing about a change in the Church's negative and prohibitory attitude toward the use of mechanical and chemical means of contraception. For the most part, the discussion was quiet and restrained. By the end of the Second Vatican Council, however, the pace and the heat of the discussion had increased and was to continue increasing thereafter. Where the primary discussants had initially been professional, clerical theologians, writing in the relative privacy of theological journals, they were soon joined by an increasing number of lay voices; and the discussion, by now a full-fledged debate, passed into the secular and the general Catholic press.

In response to the first glimmerings of debate Pope John XXIII had convened a special papal commission to deal with the subject. Later Pope Paul VI increased the size of the commission adding, in particular, a number of lay specialists. The very existence of such a papal commission was widely taken as a sign that the question of contraception was, at the least, a matter of uncertainty in the Church; at the most, it was taken as a sign that the earlier teaching, affirmed most pointedly by Pope Pius XI in his 1930 encyclical *Casti Connubii,* was in doubt and required a change. Pope Paul's commission issued its report during the spring of 1966, and it turned out that the commission was split. The majority came out in favor of a change in the Church's teaching, making no distinction between mechanical and chemical means of birth control. The minority stood fast in their support of a prohibition of contraception.

The findings of this papal commission did not become public knowledge until the spring of 1967. At that time the majority and minority reports came into the hands of the Paris daily, *Le Monde,* and subsequently appeared in an English translation in *The National Catholic Reporter.* When it became known that a majority of the commission favored a change in the Church's teaching, it was widely believed that the Pope, when he finally spoke, would have to take account of their opinion. Moreover, in the aftermath of the Council it became increasingly evident that a large number of Catholics, perhaps a majority and including both priests and laity, were in favor of a change. For an agonizingly long time, the Pope remained quiet; his expected statement did not appear. During this period of waiting, though, many had already formed their conscience and made up their minds in favor of contraception. They had listened to the arguments of Catholic theologians in favor of contraception, had recognized that the papal delay bespoke an actual state of uncertainty, and had found the moral reasons for using contraceptives overwhelming.

Then came the beginning of the second era. That

occurred with the publication of Pope Paul's encyclical. It is impossible to exaggerate the surprise the encyclical caused. It flew in the face of the Pope's own commission, whose conclusions were specifically rejected by the Pope. It flew in the face of an emergent consensus of theologians. It flew in the face of a number of bishops who had asked the Pope not to issue such an encyclical and who had already told their people they should do as their informed consciences dictated. Finally, and most importantly, it flew in the face of a great mass of married lay people. On the basis of their own marital experience and fortified by their knowledge of a change in the thinking of many bishops, priests and theologians, they had decided they could morally use contraceptives for the sake of responsible parenthood.

The trend then witnessed, and which continues, was a massive and public dissent from the encyclical. This dissent encompassed a great number of priests, many of whom risked rebuke and suspension (which many promptly got), and countless lay people. It also became known that a significant number of bishops privately protested to the Pope over the encyclical and that a number of national hierarchies (particularly the Canadian, Austrian, English, German and Belgian ones) issued statements that affirmed the individual's right to follow an informed personal conscience on contraception. Clearly the Church had on its hands a crisis of authority the likes of which it had not seen for centuries. And just as clearly those lay Catholics who had come to see the morality of contraception, but who wanted also to respect the authority of the Pope, were faced with a private crisis of conscience. It was the

public crisis of authority that captured the headlines:
The spectacle of strong petitions and statements against
the encyclical, the suspension of a number of priests,
the Pope's insistently repeated defense of the encyclical
and condemnation of dissenters, occasional sit-ins and
walk-outs were all dramatic and newsworthy.

This book is not particularly concerned with the
drama of that crisis and its long-range meaning for the
function and status of papal authority. Instead, its concern is with the quieter, usually unknown wrestling of
married lay people with their own consciences. At the
moment many are bewildered, even intimidated by the
Pope's encyclical. They want to do the right thing. They
want to act as Christians ought to act. They want to do
justice to their present children and those who are as
yet unborn. They want to be open to the voice of the
Holy Spirit and the legitimate voice of authority. They
want to live responsible sexual lives. They want to be
one with their Church.

For those who feel impelled—for personal, Christian,
and moral reasons—to use contraceptives, the Pope's
encyclical can only appear as an obstacle. For it says
these people will not be doing the right thing if they
use contraceptives; it says they will not be acting as
Christians ought to act; it says they will not be doing
justice to their families; it says they will be disobe-
dient to legitimate authority; it says they will be living
irresponsible sexual lives; it says they will not be united
with their Church.

I think the encyclical is wrong on all these points.
Put positively, I think there are many occasions when
Christian couples may use contraceptives and do so
with sufficient Catholic support to set their consciences

at rest. I do not say "full" Catholic support; obviously
they will get no support from the Pope and those
bishops who agree with him. But they will get *sufficient*
Catholic support: from the many dissenting theologians
and priests, from the many bishops throughout the
world who believe a Catholic must follow his own informed conscience, and from the many lay people, like
themselves, who have reached a similar conclusion.
That is, I believe, full enough Catholic support to set at
rest even the minds of the most scrupulous. Indeed,
there is an argument to be made that the Catholic case
for contraception should never receive monolithic support in the Church. There are many things not yet
known about the long-range effects of a widespread use
of contraceptives. It is conceivable that many of these
effects will turn out to be harmful. But as yet we do
not know what the effects will be and there is no special reason to fear the worst. We must work with what
we now know and form our conscience from the information, experience, and insights at hand. It will do
the Church no harm, and may someday do it some
good, that some remain resolutely opposed to contraception; different viewpoints on so complex and delicate a
matter are to be expected and welcomed.

The purpose of this book is to make available articles
and documents substantiating the contention that Catholic couples who conscientiously decide in favor of contraceptives do in fact have sufficient support for their
decision. It would have been easy to include in such a
book articles by Protestants, Jews, and others in favor
of contraception. Their moral insights and prodding
have been of great value to Catholics. But my intention
is to help show that one need not leave the confines of

the Catholic community to get the support he or she may feel necessary. As such, I hope the book will be useful for couples who would like to see the evidence of support before their eyes; for doctors, confessors, and counselors who may be called upon for advice; and for the general public, which might like some idea why many Catholics have been led in the direction of affirming the morality of contraception. Both the title of the book and most of its contents display the side it has chosen; it is not meant to present "both sides" of the case. At the same time, I would not like my own book to exemplify that monolithic spirit I have just finished deploring. Hence, I have included the encyclical itself as well as the minority report of the papal commission. Needless to say, both should be read, though I would also add that nothing they say seems to me strong enough to overcome the cumulative power of the articles I have chosen.

I have organized the book into three parts. The first part reprints articles and excerpts by John T. Noonan, Jr., Father Charles E. Curran, Julian Pleasants, and Sidney Callahan. They were all written prior to the encyclical. Professor Noonan's article discusses the state of the question as the Council Fathers envisaged it by the end of the Council. Later, after the publication of the encyclical, he joined the public dissenters. Father Curran's article was chosen because I think it sets out beautifully and graphically how he, as a professional moral theologian, gradually came to change his mind. His leadership in formulating and circulating the theologians' statement of dissent after the encyclical (see p. 67) suggests the depth of conviction he has manifested since that change. Sidney Callahan's article presents a conspectus of Christian-Catholic arguments in favor of contraception.

The second part encompasses dissenting reactions to the encyclicals. The theologians' statement, signed by over six hundred Catholic scholars and teachers in the fields of theology and philosophy, succinctly summarizes all the varied objections to the contents of the encyclical. Father Gregory Baum points out how the theology of Catholic authority itself permits dissent from the encyclical. Father Bernard Häring, probably the Church's most distinguished and influential moral theologian, reveals some important information behind the issuance of the encyclical and also makes evident his own reasons for dissent. Michael Novak and Mary Perkins Ryan, two influential lay theologians who did much to bring the issue of contraception to public attention, detail the response they think Catholics now should make to the encyclical. Dr. Thomas Draper, a practicing obstetrician and a public health official, speaks to the problem from his moral-professional perspective. Reprinted here also is an editorial that appeared in *The National Catholic Reporter* just after the publication of the encyclical.

The third section comprises the majority and minority reports of the papal birth control commission and the Pope's encyclical itself.

It would not be amiss to end this brief introduction with an autobiographical note. As the father of six children, I do not come to the subject of contraception as a disinterested observer. It is an intensely personal issue. I have, if you will, a spiritual stake in finding and proclaiming Catholic support for dissent from the encyclical and support for the use of contraceptives. My wife (Sidney Callahan) and I decided about three years ago that it was moral for a Catholic couple in many circumstances to limit the size of their family and to use those methods which seem most reliable. That decision was very long in the making and very hard. As short a time ago as 1964 my wife and I both wrote, in anonymous essays in Michael Novak's book *The Experience of Marriage* (Macmillan), that we had no problems with rhythm and that we could live with the teaching against contraception.

That situation rapidly changed thereafter. The "major problems" we stated we did not have at that time soon put in their appearance. And like others we began reading and thinking more seriously about the case being put forward by other Catholics in favor of contraception. I think I can honestly say that it was almost exclusively these Catholics arguments which changed our minds. Unlike many Catholic couples, my wife and I both grew up in small families and we both decided that, for our part, we wanted a large family. And also, unlike many Catholic couples, we received most of our education at non-Catholic schools and universities. For years, as our family grew larger, we lived in a resolutely secular atmosphere prone to snicker at large families. We were not impressed with the snickers and the frequently cutting remarks. To this day we retain a distaste for those self-righteous, all-knowing people who think it the essence of enlightenment to have exactly the number of children one wants exactly when one wants them. There is, in our judgment, such a thing as a "contraceptive mentality" among many, and it is not nice to behold. Its main characteristic is that of looking upon an unexpected or "unwanted" child as an unmitigated disaster, a threat to middle-class affluence, enlightened self-fulfillment, and the well-controlled, well-ordered managing of one's affairs. The great virtue of the position enunciated in Pope Paul's encyclical is that it does provide a spiritual and emotional context for accepting and loving the unexpected and even initially unwanted child. There remains a place in this active, tightly organized world of ours for passivity and acceptance, and this is true of procreation as well. But there is also, and just as importantly, a place for the responsible use of contraceptives. For all these reasons, only the Catholic arguments in favor of contraception made a real difference. Not because the non-Catholic arguments were, in themselves, defective; many have now been incorporated into the Catholic perspective. Rather, in this case, we were interested in those arguments that took full account of the Catholic tradition and some central Catholic values. None of the articles I have presented in this book supports a "contraceptive mentality" as I have defined it, none supports indifference or casualness toward contraception and responsible parenthood, and none is scornful of papal authority as such. There are many good moral reasons for the use of contraceptives in a variety of circumstances. But the reasons likely to prove most persuasive to Catholics are those achieved by their fellow Catholics. That is what is presented here. One final point ought to be made absolutely clear: *The Catholic Case for Contraception* is a case for freedom of responsible choice. It is not a case that implies that people *ought* to use contraceptives, much less to lay down general rules specifying *when* they ought to use them. It is only a case that says that there *may be* occasions when their use will seem morally wise and that it is up to individual couples, sensitive to conscience, to make their own final decision.

DANIEL CALLAHAN

Hastings-on-Hudson, N. Y.
October 1968

Part I

1

Contraception and the Council [*]

————◆◆◆————

John T. Noonan, Jr.

Vatican II stated expressly that as to contraception "the Holy Synod does not intend to propose concrete solutions directly." The reason was also given: "certain questions which need other and more searching inquiries have been given, by command of the Supreme Pontiff, to the Commission for the Study of Population, Family, and Natality." The question of contraceptive practice was thus recognized to be outside the Council's domain of action. This frank recognition of a limit, and the delicate, nuanced, and balanced language of Schema XIII, the conciliar document on marriage in the modern world, has obscured the substantial development of doctrine which the Council effected. The Council did not propose concrete solutions "directly." It did provide a fresh analysis of values, a new framework of concepts,

* From *Commonweal*, March 11, 1966.

and a recasting of past teaching, in terms of which concrete solutions might be sought.

The significance of the Council's teaching appears
most strongly if it is set against two backgrounds: the
background of the previous nineteen hundred years of
Church teaching on marriage and marital intercourse;
and the immediate background of conciliar drafts and
amendments from which the final text emerged. The
basic council document was prepared by a special subcommittee of the conciliar Commissions on Doctrine
and the Lay Apostolate, of which Bernard Häring,
C.SS.R., was secretary. This document of April, 1964,
was then thoroughly revised as to language but not as to
substance by another subcommittee of these Commissions in the summer of 1965.

The revised document was accepted on November 16,
1965, by the Council by a vote of 1,596 to 72, but with
484 Fathers favoring amendments (*modi*). According
to the rules of the Council these *modi* could be accepted only if they did not go against the substance of
the document. Their acceptability was passed on by the
Mixed Commission, consisting of thirty bishops from
the Commission on the Lay Apostolate and thirty
bishops from the Commission on Doctrine. Reference
here will be made to these accepted or rejected amendments by the number—m.1, m.2, etc.—they bear in the
printed legislative history of the Council. Only in these
contexts of past history and immediate legislative struggle can one perceive clearly the balances struck, the
blendings achieved, the nuances preserved, and the tri-
umphs accomplished.

That the teaching of Vatican II should be of the
greatest relevance to Catholic doctrine on contraception

is not surprising when it is remarked that the Second
Vatican Council was the first council in the history of
the Church to speak on the purposes of marital intercourse. This subject, which was unmentioned in the
Gospels, had been left largely to the speculations of
the theologians. It had never been a matter of authoritative teaching by a general council, nor, I believe, by any
council. Now, for the first time, as the culmination of a
slow evolution that took a decisive turn about 1680, a
council gave authoritative teaching on coital purpose.

At various earlier times in the history of the Church
it had been the common opinion of Catholic theologians
that the only lawful purpose for initiating intercourse
was procreation; a consciously procreative intent was
required. This view, derived from the Stoics, was asserted by Clement of Alexandria, and, adopted by
Origen, played a guiding role in the Greek Church. In
the West it was affirmed by St. Ambrose, St. Jerome,
and, above all, by St. Augustine, who riveted it on
Western moral thought. From 1100 to 1680 the Alexan-
drian or Augustinian requirement of procreative purpose was dominant among Catholic moral theologians.

By the end of the fifteenth century, however, a sharp
critique had been made of the dominant theory, and
Paris theologians had suggested that among the lawful
purposes of marital coitus where the avoidance of adultery, the restoration of bodily and psychic health, and
even the achievement of pleasure. Between 1480 and
1680 there went on a major theological controversy
conducted in these categories. In 1563 the Council of
Trent for the first time spoke at a conciliar level about
love in marriage, but did not relate it to intercourse.
Yet during the next century it became accepted that

intercourse in order to avoid incontinence elsewhere was lawful; after all, this view had the implicit support of St. Paul in I Corinthians: 7. In adopting this analysis, the seventeenth-century theologians broke with the Augustinian insistence that sexual acts must be somehow tied to procreative purpose. At the same time they were uneasy about pleasure as a purpose in itself, and the consensus was that to seek pleasure only in intercourse, while excluding other purposes, was to commit venial sin.

Only in the nineteenth century was the idea advanced that the expression and fostering of love could be recognized as a purpose of marital intercourse. This thought was not developed in nineteenth century theology, although by the end of the century Alois De Smet could add the un-Tridentine thought, apropos of the love which Trent had spoken of in marriage, "The marriage act itself, by which the partners are made one flesh, cultivates and nourishes this love." Substantial theoretical development of this new, non-Augustinian insight was made in 1925 by the German layman, Dietrich Von Hildebrand, in his *Reinheit und Jungfraulichkeit,* and above all, in 1935 by the German priest, Herbert Doms in his *Vom Sinn and Zweck der Ehe.* Doms set out a complete theory of coitus as an ontological act of reciprocal love, "an act which contains the abandonment and enjoyment of the whole person and is not simply an isolated activity of organs."

Doms' theory was received with coldness, the Holy Office issuing a decree on April 1, 1944, that was interpreted as rebuking it. But his emphasis on persons, in contrast to the earlier focus on the biological act, was taken up by Pius XII in 1949 in an allocution condemn-

ing artificial insemination. In the 1950's, a position
balancing procreation and conjugal love was set out by
the leading moral theologians, Bernard Häring and
Joseph Fuchs. Marital intercourse, Häring said, was "a
fundamental mediation of charity." Apart from procreation, one of its permissible purposes was "the augmen-
tation of love." The loving union of spouses, however,
was not directed to their own completion, but to the
child, whose "virtual presence" was "inscribed in the
ontological act of total union." Similarly Fuchs taught
that expression of love was a purpose of intercourse,
although this love "entirely (although not solely or as
a mere means) serves and is subordinated to the education of offspring, to whose generation such an act ex-
pressive of love is evidently ordered."

There had then already occurred in theological
thought a development which, blending procreation and
conjugal love, recognized both as purposes of intercourse. Vatican II confirmed and crowned this development by relating the coital expression of conjugal love
to procreation, but also giving such expression a substantial value independent of procreation. Conjugal
love, the Council now taught, had its origin from God's
invitation to the married to love each other, and the
Lord had "cleansed, perfected, and elevated" this love.
Such love is "directed from person to person" and "com-
pletes the good of the whole person." This was Doms
on the ontological significance of coitus. Such "emi-
nently human love," the Council continued, "is able to
enrich the expressions of the body and of the spirit with
a peculiar dignity and ennoble them as elements and
special signs of conjugal friendship."

The Council then went on to teach specifically. "This

love is singularly expressed and perfected by the proper
work of marriage. The acts, then, by which the spouses
intimately and chastely unite with each other are decent
and worthy, and exercised in a truly human way, signify and foster a mutual giving by which with joyful
and grateful spirit they reciprocally enrich each other"
(sec.49 of Schema XIII, *The Church in the Modern
World*).

One Father sought to excise the final clause running
from "by which" to "enrich each other." His amendment was rejected by the Mixed Commission with the
comment, "This sentence was expressly and pressingly
asked for by the laymen" (m.57). Four Fathers sought
to replace "perfected" in the first clause by "consum-
mated." The amendment was rejected on the ground
that "perfected" "brings the human aspect better into
the light" (m.55). In short, the Council insisted that
the coital act was human and personal, enriching the
persons involved, and remarkably expressing the love
which the Lord had perfected.

This insistence on the great value of love as an end
of intercourse was a far cry from Clement, Augustine,
and the dominant theological teaching of pre-seven-
teenth-century Catholic thought. Not only was love set
forth as an excellent purpose. The classification of primary and secondary ends in marriage—a classification
often used in debates on contraception—was deliberately rejected. Marriage, the Council said, was endowed
by God "with various goods and ends" (sec.47). Family life was said to be a good of marriage, "not putting
second the other ends of marriage" (sec.50). Two
Fathers objected that for these reasons the whole chapter "was still theologically immature, equivocal and

reticent in certain essentials: it insists predominantly and almost uniquely on conjugal love and on personal donation, which they say does not correspond to the way of speaking of the Church from earliest times." At least, these Fathers said, the chapter ought to speak of "the hierarchy of ends" and "the intrinsic malice of onanism" (m.1). One hundred and ninety Fathers asked that the text be amended "to recall Catholic doctrine up till now handed down and to better indicate the hierarchy of ends" (m.16). Another Father proposed the amendment, "Conjugal love is ordained to the primary end of marriage, which is offspring" (m.72).

All of these attempts to insert the hierarchy of ends were defeated. The Mixed Commission said laconically, "It may be noted that the hierarchy of goods can be considered under different aspects." Brusquer treatment was given an arch-conservative attempt to reaffirm Augustine by saying "conjugal love, independent of the intention of procreating offspring, does not justify the conjugal act." This, the Mixed Commission said, "does not square with received doctrine" (m.67). The rejected amendments here, like the rejected amendments to the conciliar decree on religious liberty, stand as forlorn monuments to a theology which has been passed by.

Conjugal love, however, was not left unrelated to procreation and education. Here Häring and Fuchs were followed. "By its natural character, the very institution of marriage and conjugal love are ordained to the procreation and education of offspring as they are crowned by their birth" (sec.48; cf. sec.50). The Council declared this twice, adding the second time this amendment, "Truly children are a most excellent gift of marriage and contribute especially to the good of the

parents themselves." As the Mixed Commission pointed
out, the "primordial importance of procreation and
education is at least ten times expounded in the text"
(m.15). Procreation and education were said to be
cooperation in the work of the Creator; responsible
procreation was said to be itself the generous fulfilling
of a duty imposed on spouses. Not only was the procreative value strongly affirmed, but the Council also
found "worthy of particular commendation" those who
raised "a larger number of offspring to be appropriately
educated" (sec.50).

In Short, the Council affirmed strongly and insistently
that procreation was good and that marriage was directed to it. At the same time, in complete accord with
classical Catholic expositions of the goods of marriage,
procreation was never separated from education, except arguably in the amendment on the excellence of
children; yet even this amendment was probably controlled by the sentence which preceded it and spoke of
the "procreation and education of children." There
cannot be found in the conciliar exposition any attempt
to praise uncontrolled procreation or to assert that
procreation, apart from education, is good.

The coordinate emphasis on procreation and education was related to the stress the Council laid on parental responsibility to determine the number of children.
Here the Council was summing up theological writing
of the 1950's, but at the same time setting a precedent
in being the first Council to speak to the issue. In the
April, 1964, draft of Schema XIII this responsibility was
put very strongly: "Christian spouses know they are not
the slaves of blind instinct." On the floor of the Council
in November, 1964, Cardinal Ottaviani challenged this

stress on parental responsibility as a dangerous novelty. Yet the revised text, no longer containing the sentence on blind instinct, was scarcely less emphatic than the first draft. The Council said that each couple was to decide the number of children they should have. They were to make the decision "attending both to their own good and the good of their children whether now born or to be born, diagnosing both the temporal and spiritual conditions of the times and their state of life, and taking into account the good of the family community, temporal society, and the Church itself" (sec.50).

This affirmation was scarcely tempered by the following statement that in making the decision the couple were to be "docile toward the magisterium." The magisterium had never taught how many children a couple should have. Indeed it now taught, through the mouth of the Council, that a context of multiple goods was the framework in which a decision as to offspring should be made. What the Council regarded as relevant in making this decision was far broader than what Pius XII in 1951 had conceded in his Allocution to the Midwives could provide reason for regulating births—that is, "medical, eugenic, economic, and social" motives. Now the Christian couple were told explicitly by the magisterium to consider their own good, their family good, and their state of life; and there was unmistakable reference to the value to which procreation was invariably wedded, education, when the Council told parents to consider the good of their children born and to be born. "This judgment," the Council said of the judgment as to number, "must ultimately be made before God by the spouses themselves" (sec.50). The Mixed Commission struck from this sentence the concluding words "and

by no one else" because these words "could seem too
harsh" and might exclude advice; but the Commission
acted with the explicit caution that the sense of the sentence, "by which every undue intervention is excluded,"
was unchanged. The word "ultimately" was retained
over objection, because "it underlines the proper responsibility of the spouses" (m.81).

What relevance to contraception had these strong
conciliar affirmations on conjugal love as a purpose of
intercourse, on the linked goods of procreation and education, and on ultimate parental responsibility? The
Council began to relate the basic goods and contraception in section 51, "The reconciling of conjugal love
with respect for human life." The Council said it knew
that "often in conditions of today's life," spouses are in
circumstances "in which the number of offspring, at any
rate for the time being, cannot be increased." The
parental responsibility to limit births then conflicted
with the demands of love, and this conflict, the Council
noted, threatened both the good of marital fidelity and
the education of the children. There was candid avowal
that the attempt to achieve all the basic goods of marriage might produce a crisis.

Recognizing the difficulty, the Council went on to
say "There are those who presume to offer to these
problems indecent solutions; indeed they do not shrink
from killing." To such persons, the Council declared
that life "from conception" was to be guarded with the
greatest care. This statement was itself a doctrinal advance at the level of conciliar statement; no Council
before had spoken so clearly as to the instant from
which the embryo demanded respect. "Abortion and
infanticide," the council affirmed, "are horrible crimes."

There were also, the Council taught, moral criteria for marital coitus. These criteria are "taken from the nature of the person and his acts." These criteria must determine what acts respect "an integral sense of mutual donation and human procreation in the context of true love." In these statements a true advance occurred. Rejected was the scholastic approach rooted in St. Thomas which stated that the criteria were to be found in the nature of the act of coitus. One hundred and nine Fathers had sought to state the acts expressing married love in the old scholastic terms of "acts per se apt for the generation of offspring." This hallowed formula was sharply rejected by the Mixed Commission with the decisive comment, "Not all acts tend to generation (cf. sterility and the sterile times)" (m.56).

Now, in setting out the objective criteria of birth regulation, thirteen Fathers asked that "criteria" be modified with the words "as, e.g., in the generative faculty of human nature founded in the same dignity of the human person." This attempt to emphasize the generative faculty was rejected by the Mixed Commission (m.104). Also rejected was the amendment offered by one Father to add after the words "human procreation" the old scholastic formula "and the natural ordination of the act" (m.105). In sharp contrast, the Mixed Commission chose the words "taken from the nature of the person and his acts" because "by these words it is asserted that the acts are not to be judged according to a merely biological aspect, but as they relate to the human person integrally and adequately considered" (m.104). In accepting this criterion, the Council eliminated the usual scholastic arguments against contraception which were focused on the nature of the coital act abstracted from the person. Now the person and all his acts—educational as well as generative—were made the norm for judgment.

In the language used by the Council there was a reminiscence of the argument advanced by Doms that contraception hindered the ontological gift of oneself in coitus. "If a person," Doms had said, "mutilates the biological process anatomically or physiologically, before, during, or after the act, he only gives himself with an arbitrary reservation, which is contrary to the immutable meaning of the sexual act and the most profound intention of conjugal love." The Council, however, did not adopt this argument. It left open the possibility that this argument might, however, be a valid objection, at least to those contraceptive acts destroying the physical integrity of coitus.

Attached to the April, 1964, draft of Schema XIII there had been an Appendix where it was explicitly stated that "Every deliberate intervention of men which vitiates the work proper to the conjugal act of the person is contrary to divine law and the order of matrimony; nor can such a way of acting be consonant with the integrity of conjugal love." Here was an express condemnation of coitus interruptus and the condom. A proposed footnote buttressed the text by noting that these methods were condemned by *Casti Connubii*. In the revised draft these references to particular contraceptive means were dropped.

In this final refusal to speak out on any contraceptive means, the Council refrained from judgment on any of them. It had stated in the introduction to the chapter on marriage that marriage today was profaned by "illicit practice against generation." But "such practices" were not made precise; oral and anal intercourse could have been meant. The Mixed Commission had rejected an effort to say "contraceptive arts" at this point instead of "illicit practices." It did so for the pointed reason that "contraceptive arts" could include "the method of periodic continence, which often requires technical computations" (m.51).

The final draft, like the April, 1964, text, contained a reference to *Casti Connubii* and to the precise pages where *Casti Connubii* condemned contraceptive means interrupting the coital act. This reference was added, in the end, in an amendment called to the Mixed Commission's attention by the Cardinal Secretary of State. But, unlike the April, 1964, draft, it was no longer said that the Council endorsed the condemnation. *Casti Connubii* became a footnote, introduced by "cf." It was a footnote attached to the clause "ways reproved by the magisterium when it explains the divine law." The footnote then asked the reader to "refer to" *Casti Connubii*. Did this cryptic notation mean that the Council was teaching that *Casti Connubii* was a case where the magisterium had stated divine law? Hardly, because the footnote reference to *Casti Connubii* was amplified by further references: to Pius XII's 1951 Allocution to the Midwives, and to Paul VI's Allocution to the Cardinals of June 23, 1964. The Allocution to the Midwives expanded *Casti Connubii* by saying it condemned attempts to impede procreation by preventing the "development of the natural consequences" of conjugal intercourse; in short, it condemned the diaphragm and douche. Paul VI's Allocution to the Cardinals, a reference added by the Mixed Commission, referred to "birth control" in general and said, "We must say openly that up to now

we have not sufficient reason to consider the norms
given by Pius XII in this matter to be out of date
[*superate*] and therefore not binding." These were to
bind "at least until we feel in conscience obliged to
modify them," because "in a matter of such importance
it seems good that Catholics wish to observe a single
law." The norms given by Pius XII were probably those
he had given on the progesterone pill in 1958, but arguably they included his 1951 teaching to the Midwives.
Surely "norms" "given" by a Pope which might be
shown to be "out of date" were not meant as divine
law; and if the Council was not teaching by its elusive
footnote 14 that the rules of Pius XII on the pill, douche
and diaphragm were divine law, it could not be consistently argued that it was teaching that *Casti Connubii*
on the condom and coitus interruptus was divine law.

Indeed, the most striking aspect of the Council on
contraception was the way that it put the existing law
on contraception as law for "children of the Church."
Pius XI had taught very strongly in *Casti Connubii* that
the contraceptive acts condemned therein were contrary to the good of any man, Christian or pagan. The
Council did not repudiate this teaching, because in its
general deploring of the illicit practices against generation and in its setting out of objective moral criteria
based on the person, it was speaking to all men, too.
Indeed the introductory section of the marriage chapter noted that the Council "intends to illuminate and
comfort all men." Yet, when the Council turned to existing discipline in the Church on contraception, it
ceased to talk of all men. Rather it said that "for children of the Church" "it is not lawful" to use methods of
regulating procreation which "have been reproved by

the magisterium when it interprets the divine law." The footnote reference to Paul VI's Allocution to the Cardinals showed that the Council believed that in the process of interpreting divine law a Pope could give norms which were open to revision but which should be obeyed as authoritative teaching until revised. In short, the casting of the teaching on contraception in terms of what was not lawful, and the application of this teaching only to Catholics, would seem to suggest that the Council viewed existing condemnations as, at least in part, open to revision. In this it was in perfect harmony with Paul VI who thought it desirable that, until they were revised by him, a single law should bind Catholics.

Finally, the Council gave some guidance as to how conjugal love and the education of children were to be reconciled with the responsibility to regulate the number of offspring. It stated flatly "that there cannot be a true contradiction between the divine laws of transmitting life and those favoring genuine conjugal love." When those were known it would also be known what rules could not be divine law. At least such a procedure seemed recommended by the Council in preference to one of hypothesizing the divine laws and trying to accommodate the laws of conjugal love to them.

The Council, subtly but decisively, indicated by example and precept its preference for the first method. It began the chapter on marriage by the statement that it proceeded not only in the light of the Gospels but "in the light of the human experience of all men." The Council itself meant to rely on human testimony as to the requirements of love. Looking specifically "to the necessities and advantages of the family which are

appropriate for the new day," the Council declared
that a great contribution might be made by "the Christian sense of the faithful." Six Fathers wished to qualify
this appeal to the faithful by qualifying the sense of
the faithful as "showing filial obedience to the magisterium of the Church." The Mixed Commission re-
sponded that enough had been said of the magisterium
(m.113). What the Council valued was the *consensus
fidelium;* as the Council had earlier taught in its Constitution on the Church, "The holy people of God share
also in Christ's prophetic office." Beyond this invocation
of the witness of the faithful, the Council asked scientists "to try to elucidate more deeply the different
conditions favoring the decent regulation of human procreation." Again there was no assumption that all the
divine and natural laws on birth regulation were known
to the Council or even to the well-read theologian. The
appeal was to empirical investigation to discover the
conditions.

The Council, then, has not proposed solutions "directly," as to how conjugal love and parental responsibility may be reconciled. It has, however, set up the
main pillars of any solution: procreation and education
are indissolubly linked goods; conjugal love is in itself
a legitimate and laudable purpose of intercourse; em-
bryonic life is to be guarded; the dignity of the person
is to provide norms; there is an element of divine law
in previous teaching by the Church on contraception,
but not all existing law on contraception is immutable.
Solutions for the new day are to be found both by discerning what is divine and immutable and by consult-
ing experts and the Christian faithful.

Personal Reflections
on Birth Control *

—————◆◆◆—————

Charles E. Curran

. . . I have added my own "Amen" to those who are asking for a change in the present teaching of the Church. Why the change?

My arguments in favor of the present teaching of the Church developed along the lines of the controlling and directing influence of love with regard to sexuality. The present teaching of the Church emphasizes the dignity and spiritual freedom of man who controls and determines his whole life. The spiritual core of man guides and gives intelligibility to the material part of human nature. Contraception, by not directly appealing to the higher forces of love and control, could easily enclose man in the realm of the purely material. Sacrifice and control will always be a part of man's life. True Chris-

* From *Christian Morality Today*, Fides, 1966.

tian asceticism does not constrain the individual; rather it enables the Christian to participate ever more in the freedom of the children of God which only the life-giving Spirit can produce. Like Christ, man dies to self and rises in the newness of life.

A brief reflection shows that the position outlined above is more of a defense than an argument. The reasoning assumes the present teaching of the Church and then tries to explain it within the whole context of the Paschal Mystery which is the basis of all Christian life. But theologians cannot merely assume the truth of the present teaching of the Church. Is such love and control an essential element of Christian marriage?

Contact and dialogue with many married Christians forced me to reconsider my views. Many couples found themselves in the dilemma of realizing a need to express their love in a human way and yet dared not have any more children. Family love and marriages were weakened and at times almost destroyed because couples could not fully express their love in a sexual way. The question arose almost instinctively—would such a couple be breaking their relationship with God by using contraception? In some cases I was sure that the couple would not be guilty of mortal sin.

Some had taken the risk and decided to use contraception. Many other conscientious non-Catholic Christians are doing the same. Are they breaking their relationship with God? How can I tell? The criterion frequently proposed in scripture is the love of our neighbor. How can we love the God we do not see if we cannot love our neighbor whom we do see? The last judgment as portrayed in Matthew's account bases man's relationship with God on his relationship with his fellow men. "For when I was hungry, you gave me food; when thirsty, you gave me drink. . . ." (Matt. 25:31–46). Some people using contraception are most generous in their love of God and neighbor. A good number have followed the teaching of the Church, but now find that their marriage, their health, and their finances persuade them not to have any more children. They are devoted husbands and wives, fathers and mothers; they give of their few moments of free time in projects for the betterment of society; they are kind to all; they go out of their way to help others; they try to overcome their feelings of vengeance and rancor. By their fruits you will know them. They seem to be good Christians who have not broken their relationship with God.

Theologians have always admitted that something can be objectively sinful even though for a particular person because of subjective circumstances it might not be a subjective sin. But the frequency of the subjective occurrence does raise doubts about the objective sinfulness. My attention focused on three aspects connected with the present teaching of the Church: human sexuality, the nature of the moral judgment, the authority and teaching of the popes.

Does the present teaching of the Church reflect the complex reality of human sexuality? Through their sexual union husband and wife express and intensify their union of love. Three influences—comparatively recent medical knowledge, various theological aberrations, and a celibate attitude toward sexuality—have tended to give a rather distorted notion of sexuality.

For centuries the lack of biological and medical knowledge made it impossible for man to separate procreation and sexuality. St. Alphonsus, the eighteenth-century patron of moral theologians and confessors, followed the biological concepts of Aristotle and Galen. The uterus was the nest in which the child developed. The woman contributed certain fluids or even a type of semen which mixed with the male semen in the uterus, coagulated, became frothy, and evolved into the embryo. New scientific discoveries, aided by the invention of the microscope, expanded medical knowledge in the late seventeenth century. For example, de Graaf proposed the evidence that the female testes are ovaries, and he described the follicles that ever since have been associated with his name. Only with the work of Ogino and Knaus (1929–1930) did man become certain of the comparatively short time in a female cycle when a woman is fertile. Until a hundred years ago, inadequate medical knowledge led theologians to believe that every sexual union was connected with the real possibility of procreation. The science of theology in accepting the theological principles of older theologians has also, perhaps unconsciously, accepted a rather one-sided concept of sexuality.

The theological aberrations of Gnosticism, Jansenism, and all others that look down on the material part of man have tended to overemphasize the procreative aspect of sexuality. For many centuries it was the intention of procreation which alone completely justified marital intercourse. Theories proposing the evil of matter concentrate on sexuality. Many zealots falsely interpreted the Pauline dichotomy of flesh and spirit in an ontological sense as the war between the spiritual and the material in man. Today theology has a renewed consciousness of the value of earthly realities.

Matter is not bad; it is a part of the order of creation and the order of the redemption through the Paschal Mystery. Sexuality no longer appears as an evil which is tolerated for the purpose of procreation.

My own celibacy puts me at a disadvantage in considering marital sexuality. There is no experimental knowledge of the meaning of sexuality in marriage. In addition, a celibate mentality can easily form a warped concept of sexuality in marriage. I too was trained in the idea that the pleasures of sex make up for the burdens of marriage. Masturbation thus appears as the starting point for a theology of marital sexuality! Even though I reject such a concept of sexuality, I have still been influenced by it. A celibate attitude does tend to see sexuality only in the light of pleasure and procreation.

Today theologians acknowledge the love-union aspect of marital sexuality. In fact, the love-union aspect of sexuality "justifies" marital sexuality when procreation is impossible. With the acceptance of rhythm, it seems that the Church has admitted the love-union value of sexuality as a value in its own right apart from procreation. Seen in such a light, contraception does not differ that much from rhythm. It is true that sexuality must always be an expression and intensification of love, but conscientious husbands and wives should know best the demands of love in their own lives.

The moral judgment is the final and ultimate judgment, reducing, as it were, all the other aspects of the question. The moral judgment presupposes all the other considerations bearing on a particular problem—the sociological, psychological, pedagogical, hygienic, etc. Every other consideration is partial and particular with regard to the moral consideration. The moral judgment considers all the various aspects and then arrives at its final judgment. In most moral judgments some particular value (not a moral one as such) might have to be sacrificed for the good of the whole. Nothing in this world is perfect from every conceivable point of view. Every other aspect of the problem is relative to the final moral judgment. What if the biological integrity of the marital act destroys such other considerations as the educational, the love union of the spouses, the psychic and physical health of the spouses?

It seems that only in our own times has the consideration of biological integrity interfered with the other aspects that enter into the final moral judgment. Previously the cruel forces of disease and famine made the problem of family planning much less acute. Likewise, an agrarian culture was more in keeping with larger families than our highly industrialized civilization. The formation and growth of Planned Parenthood in the present century indicate that the recognition of the problem of family planning has come about only recently. Catholic theologians have popularized the expression "responsible parenthood" only in the last decade. Perhaps in earlier times the biological integrity of the marital act did not interfere with other values. But today the biological integrity must be considered together with the love-union aspect of sexuality, the health of the partners, the proper education of the children, and demographic circumstances. The biological aspect is not an absolute; it is a partial and relative consideration in the process of formulating the final moral judgment.

As human beings we experience our own inadequate knowledge and the selfish promptings from the effects of original sin in us. Man realizes his need for guidance and direction. On the other hand, the teaching authority of the Church on birth control is not infallible, not a matter of faith. The condemnation of contraception belongs to the ordinary, authentic magisterium of the Church to which we owe obedience. The very fact that the Church has not spoken infallibly indicates that the present teaching is open to development.

To change the present teaching of the Church would be a case of development and not a direct contradiction. Gregory Baum has compared a development on the birth control issue with the development of the Church's teaching on religious liberty (*Contraception and Holiness,* New York: Herder and Herder, 1964, pp. 311–343). The encyclicals of Pius IX and Leo XIII condemn religious liberty because of the false principles on which it is based. Pope John in *Pacem in Terris* and the Council Fathers of Vatican II have approved religious liberty. The Church still condemns the false basis of religious liberty proposed in the last century. However, the Church has recently become more conscious of the freedom of conscience of the individual in religious matters. The inviolability of the human person from external force and the freedom of the act of faith are the bases of the individual's freedom in matters of religion. The teachings of Pope John and the Council Fathers are not a contradiction but a development of the earlier teaching.

Another example: the encyclical *Mediator Dei* (1947) teaches that, "His cruel sufferings constitute the mystery from which our salvation chiefly springs." The *Constitution on the Sacred Liturgy* teaches that the Paschal Mystery is the heart of the redemption. The constitution on the liturgy reflects the theological, scriptural, and liturgical rediscovery of the resurrection in the plan of redemption. Pius XII in 1947 only reflected the thought of his own day, but there has been a growth in our understanding of the resurrection in the past two decades.

The present teaching of the Church on birth control reflects the theological consciousness of the Church at the time it was formulated. Since *Casti Connubii* (1930) the theology of the Church has given more attention to the love-union aspect of sexuality. The bitter controversy over the licitness of rhythm in the 1930's shows the whole church at that time did not have an adequate understanding of the love-union aspect of sexuality as a value in itself, completely apart from the possibility of procreation. Only in the last decade have theologians talked about the principle of responsible parenthood. Pius XI probably never heard of such a principle. The present teaching of the Church reflects the connection between sexuality and procreation. The project of marriage will always be procreative. But it does not seem that the present teaching of the Church reflects the demands of responsible parenthood and the love-union aspect of sexuality.

A consideration of three ideas—sexuality, the moral judgment, and the teaching authority of the Church— have influenced me to change my thinking on the present teaching of the Church on contraception. The question completely transcends the discussion about the pill. Those who advocate the use of the pill generally argue within the framework of the same categories that theologians have used with regard to marital sexuality. Now the Church must reconsider the categories and principles themselves. The proposal to change the present teaching of the Church on contraception is not a capitulation to situation ethics and a denial of any objectivity. Moral theology today does need a more personalist approach. But the proposal for a change is based on the need for a more exhaustive, objective consideration. I do not believe that the present teaching of the Church properly reflects all the objectivity in the complex reality of marital sexuality.

Both the thought and tone of the present essay are personal. I have not attempted to give a scientific and detailed argumentation; rather, I have tried to show why I have changed my own thinking. Pope Paul has pointed out the complexity and the gravity of the problem. The Pope concluded his statement by saying, "And therefore it seems opportune to recommend that no one, for the present, takes it on himself to make pronouncements in terms different from the prevailing norm." The present essay is in no way a pronouncement; it is a highly personal reflection. Nor am I advocating in practice a norm "different from the prevailing norm." My own rethinking of the subject only makes me more aware of my own limitations and less prone to make any pronouncements whatsoever.

As a confessor and guide I must continue to uphold the present teaching of the Church. In and through their marriage a Christian couple must live the gift of the Paschal Mystery. Married Christians are not second-class citizens; they are called to perfection. I stress the primacy of love in their lives. In giving marriage instructions I will spend the entire first talk on the Sermon on the Mount with its emphasis on love of others and dying to self.

The counsellor should suggest practical ways of showing marital love; e.g., the husband comes home from work and, instead of burying himself in the paper or TV screen, takes the time to share his day with his wife. Love is the most important element in their marriage. Their sexual union must be an expression and intensification of their union of love in the service of life. Young couples should be reminded of the need for responsible parenthood. I point out that rhythm with the help of a competent doctor and the use of the thermometer is more reliable than many people believe. But it is a real sacrifice for a woman trying to take her temperature when she first awakens and the children are crying and/or fighting in their bedroom. Love becomes very practical on occasion.

However, it could be that in a particular case for a particular couple in their individual circumstances the use of contraceptives might not break their relationship with God. Theologians have always admitted that in certain circumstances there might not be subjective guilt. Chancery officials today frequently imply that suicides are not guilty of grave sin. No confessor believes that all the acts of masturbation confessed by adolescents are subjectively serious sins. A couple might come to the conclusion that in their particular circumstances contraception is needed to preserve very important values in their lives.

The ultimate judgment must always be made by the individual couple. I try to see from their whole life if they have broken their relationship with God. I apply the criteria mentioned in first part of the essay with regard to their relationships with one another, with their family, their fellow workers, their neighbors, and their enemies. The fact they have made a real effort in the past would argue for their good faith. I encourage them to continue building up their relationship with God and each other. The decision to use contraception is difficult and risky. The danger of self-deception is ever present, but there are times when contraception might be necessary for an individual couple. I have counselled couples along these lines.

The complexity of the problem of birth control is evident. Since my consideration of the problem has completely neglected many aspects of the question, I dare not make any pronouncements. We must all admire the wisdom of the Pope in setting up a special commission to investigate the varied aspects of the teaching of the Church on marriage. But we must also recognize the complex circumstances that enter into the judgment made by an individual couple.

A Biologist
Asks Some Questions [*]

◆◆◆

Julian Pleasants

Biologically speaking, what makes a species a success is survival. In the long run, whatever helps a species survive is good, whatever seriously threatens its survival is bad. If the biologist, on religious or philosophical grounds, considers the survival of the human species a good thing, then generally speaking, he also accepts as good those things necessary for its survival, and he opposes behavior which threatens its survival. A biologist, therefore, is quite sensitive to the type of argument early advanced against birth control, that it is a form of race suicide. Such a possibility deserves the most serious biological consideration, and would very well justify the cautious stance taken by all the churches when birth control first became a matter of public concern. Until

[*] From *Marriage,* June, 1967.

evidence became available to show that birth control was not a threat to human survival, an uncritical acceptance of it would have been an abdication of moral responsibility.

Yet this basically biological question about birth control is seldom heard any more. Emphasis has shifted to the grounds that artificial birth control is wrong because it deliberately frustrates a natural function of the act of intercourse. To the biologists, this argument is totally incomprehensible, since he knows that life depends on the ability of an organism to suppress one function of a multi-functional act when only the other functions are needed. In an evolving world, new functions were often added on to old actions, rather than entrusted to a new type of action. This is true of such basic actions as breathing, eating, circulating the blood, and clearing the blood of wastes. Each act performs a number of functions, and various suppressive mechanisms are available in the body to see that only those functions needed at the time are carried out. If this were not so, the body would have to choose between too much of some things and not enough of others. Either choice could be fatal in many situations, since the body's survival depends on a delicate balance in the amounts of various metabolic materials.

There is no reason why the same pattern cannot apply to actions which affect society as well as the individual. In human beings a social function of stabilizing the family has been added on to the reproductive function of sexual intercourse. The social function is just as important for the survival and expansion of the human species as the reproductive one, since human infants must go through such a long period of dependency

and education. Just as the body depends on a balancing of its biochemical functions, the human species depends on a balancing of the social and reproductive
functions of sexual intercourse. Throughout most of
human history, the balance was achieved by a high rate
of infant mortality, which kept reproductive potential
low even when there was a high frequency of socially
valuable sexual intercourse. If, instead of relying on
bacteria, man can now achieve a balance by suppress-
ing the reproductive function part of the time, this is
only following the typical pattern of biological activity,
placing it under human rather than microbial control.

There are, therefore, no biological grounds for as-
serting that there is something unnatural about suppress-
ing one function of a multi-functional act. Only non-
biologists could think so. It is sometimes asserted that
this argument is based on philosophical rather than biological grounds. But it is the goal of philosophy to find
principles which apply over a broader range than that
of one particular science, such as biology. If a principle is false in biology, then it is not even worthy of
consideration as a possible philosophical principle. Unless we have a revelation from God indicating that the
act of sexual intercourse, alone of all human multi-
functional acts, must never have one of its functions
suppressed, then on what grounds can we say that such
suppression is intrinsically evil?

The act could still be *extrinsically* evil, and seriously
evil, if it proved in actual practice to lead to the ex-
tinction of the species. Many moralists have welcomed
the discovery of the anovulant pill because its use
seemed to avoid the condemnation of being intrinsically
evil. But from the biologist's point of view, the pill, be-

cause of its very effectiveness, creates a special possibility of danger to human survival, and the extent of this possibility needs to be carefully assessed.

Until the pill there was no method of birth control which could make sexual intercourse both fully satisfying psychologically and fully sterile physiologically. The older methods—interrupted intercourse and oral and anal intercourse—were psychologically unsatisfying, and the older attempts at chemical or mechanical control were very ineffective. The rhythm method becomes less satisfying the more effective it is, or, vice versa, becomes less effective the more satisfying it is. I use the term "satisfying" here not merely to mean the satisfaction of self-centered drives, but even more to mean the satisfaction of a desire for the expression of love and unity. Both kinds of drive formerly led to dissatisfaction with the more effective ways of achieving temporary sterility and to a willingness to risk the less effective ways. There was, therefore, no complete severance of the psychological and reproductive functions of intercourse. The desire for complete psychological satisfaction would inevitably lead to a certain level of reproduction.

There was still some question whether this level could maintain the race as long as the bacterial controls on human reproduction remained in effect. In France of the mid-nineteenth century, the widespread use of interrupted intercourse brought about such a decline in the birth rate that the population was no longer replacing itself with the high death rates then prevailing. Later in the century, however, the discovery of bacteria, and the development of modern hygiene made it possible to maintain and expand the population with a

far lower birth rate than was previously needed. Therefore methods of birth control which carried only a low
risk of pregnancy still need not threaten the survival of
the species.

In fact, the rapid reduction of the death rate through
the control of bacterial diseases, placed man in an altogether new situation. Non-biologists often think that
all animal species expand until they are using up all
their available food supply. In fact, however, this almost never happens. Many species which acted this way
probably evolved, but soon became extinct. This is because an animal's food supply is itself a living thing—a
plant or another animal—and has to have a chance to
reproduce itself. If the food organism is reduced below
the level at which it can maintain itself, then the animals dependent on it will also disappear. Therefore,
generally speaking, the animal species that survived
were those whose population levels were held down by
something other than food shortages. This other something could be infectious disease, or severe climate, or
predatory animals, or a psychosomatic effect of overcrowding on fertility.

Many species have even evolved special behavior
patterns which adjust the number of breeding pairs to
the amount of space available. Such a behavior pattern,
called territoriality, is very common in birds. The male
stakes out a territory and defends it against other males
of his species. The bird's song you hear in the spring
is his way of saying: "This is my land, this is my land."
Birds that do not get a territory do not get a chance to
mate. For each species, the size of a territory is fixed
by instinct, not by dividing the available land by the
number of birds present. In practice the instinct which

has evolved provides for a territory big enough to support a mating pair and their progeny without destroying their food supply. Even within the same species, however, different patterns may evolve according to need. A small species of iguana lizard practices territoriality in Texas, where rapid reproduction might destroy the food supply. But in Colorado, where cold winters keep the population low, the lizards feed and mate wherever they wish.

What happens when a population control is removed without being replaced by another was shown dramatically when man killed off the wolves and pumas which had held down the deer population of the Kaibab plateau. The deer increased rapidly from 4,000 to 100,000. These 100,000 deer so stripped the tree growth in their browsing range that 60,000 of them starved to death in the space of two winters. Because these deer had always lived under pressure from predatory species, they had not had to evolve any internal population control such as territoriality or a hormonal effect of overcrowding on fertility. Man was similarly dependent on bacterial "predators" to keep his population manageable until modern medicine changed the situation drastically.

Man is, of course, unique among animals in his remarkable ability to find and exploit new sources of food, and it is theoretically possible that his ability in this line could keep ahead of the population expansion made possible by modern medicine. In fact, however, this has not happened. For reasons which are more political, social, and economic than scientific, man's food production has lagged behind population expansion in recent decades. Not only food production, but the ability to provide for educational and cultural needs has been no match for the rate of population increase in some countries. To the biologist, overpopulation is not a state, but a rate. It is a rate of population growth which cannot now be matched by a sufficiently rapid increase in the necessities of human life (not food only).

In view of the generalization that population controls are usually advantageous to an animal species, the biologist would like to know why this should not also be true of man, at least in some circumstances. If man is going to "frustrate nature" by eliminating the bacterial controls on population growth which have operated for countless generations, why cannot he evolve a new form of population control, one which does not require that half his children die before reaching the age of six?

Despite the fact that the biologist's background has prepared him for an acceptance of population controls, the possibility of control opened up by the anovulant pill demands special biological consideration. Although it is not 100 per cent effective, it is already so close to that figure that many couples could conceivably remain childless without sacrificing any of the immediate psychological satisfactions of sexual intercourse. We must be prepared for the advent of a method 100 per cent effective. When that happens, the survival of the race will depend on the desire for children, rather than on the desire for sexual intercourse. Under such circumstances, can the species, in fact, survive?

The Puritan has already made up his mind on the question. Man is so corrupt that even the good he does is done for low motives, such as pleasure. If we separate the pleasure from the good, he will not do the good at all. Only forcing man to keep pleasure and good together, by the threat of hell-fire, will keep the race going.

The biologist, however, has found that necessary activities may be prompted by more than one drive. Man's eating of food is not a simple response to the taste of food. A low blood sugar will drive him to eat food he doesn't like. Intelligence and education can control his choice of food. Modern non-nutritive foods have separated the pleasurable taste of food from its nutritive value, but we do not hear of people starving to death because they fail to eat anything except non-nutritive foods.

There is no *a priori* answer to the question of whether people want children, and whether they would have children if they could have sexual intercourse without any risk of children. We know that in many underdeveloped countries the big obstacle to the spread of birth control is the fact that people want large families. But we have tended to dismiss this as a cover for the fact that they just don't want to be bothered with birth control methods. Is there really an independent desire for children, operating even in couples who have the education and the motivation to use the most effective contraceptive measures? An answer to this question can come only from surveys of the countries where such measures, and the motivation to use them, are widespread. The answer is quite surprising.

Since the development of more effective contraceptive devices, couples have not only continued to have children, but have continued wanting to have children. For the vast majority of Americans, childlessness is a tragedy, and having only one child is a misfortune. The strength of the desire for children is strikingly illustrated in an article in the August, 1966, issue of the *American Sociological Review*. A survey of American college women showed that 99 per cent of the religious women wanted two or more children, while even among non-religious women, 91 per cent wanted two or more children. The spread of contraception has not eliminated the desire for children. What it has done, as other surveys show, is eliminate the gap between the number people desire and the number they actually have. For the vast majority of Americans, children are not a price you pay for the joys of marriage. They are among the joys of marriage. Most American couples want more children than the demographers recommend to them, even when there are no religious limits to their use of birth control methods.

There is an independent desire for children, and the survival of the race does not depend on maintaining an indissoluble link between the satisfactions of intercourse and the risk of pregnancy. For the biologist, this is an experientially verified fact of the utmost importance, removing his last theoretical concern about the hazards of birth control. There are still plenty of practical problems about specific contraceptives, but these are not the concern of this discussion nor should they be the concern of theologians trying to formulate a new Catholic position on this subject. The questions they have to face are much more fundamental.

The most fundamental question a biologist has to ask about the present law of the Church (or any future law on the subject) is this: what kind of law is it? If it is based on a philosophical law about the relationship of pleasure and purpose in any action, how does this apply to an action which has more than one function? If the Church's norm is the expression of a biological law, what biological generalization is it based on? If the condemnation is a disciplinary law, a practical ordinance for the common good, then such a law could be justified on biological grounds if it proved necessary for the survival of the human race. If it were true that the species would die out unless contraception were condemned, then such a law could be justified. But this article has pointed out that an independent desire for children, coupled with the present low rate of infant mortality in developed countries, makes it possible for the human race to survive even if everyone practices contraception some of the time.

If the condemnation were a disciplinary law with an ascetical purpose, like the late lamented Friday abstinence, then its value for this purpose would need more clarification than it has yet received. Such a law would have its biological implications also, since the preservation of the marriage bond is biologically valuable for the education and emotional development of children and the sexual activity which strengthens that bond should not be curtailed for the sake of uncertain gains. There should be clear proof of the spiritual values to be achieved by a universal condemnation of contraception. Otherwise, a biologist would have grave misgivings about a law which would appear anti-biological, leading as it might to overpopulation and/or marital instability, without any clear indication of compensating gains.

If, however, the condemnation of contraception is based on a law of God with respect to human marriage which can be known by the human mind only through divine revelation, then a Catholic biologist is in the same boat as all other Catholics. His only question can be: what kinds of activity fall under the condemnation?

Thus the present doubt in the minds of the Catholic

laity, biologists and non-biologists alike, is not about
what the law *says,* but about what the law *is,* what kind
of law it is. Philosophical laws which deal with an activity so profoundly biological as human intercourse
must have a biological base. But biological laws apply
to a complex, evolving world, and do not have a fixed,
absolute character. Disciplinary laws admit of exceptions, when extreme hardship or conflicting obligations
demand them. But a divinely made, divinely revealed
law can apply universally without exception. Is this the
kind of law we have? Whether the law be maintained or
modified, we must be told what kind of law it is.

4

Procreation and Control *

Sidney Callahan

Conceiving, bearing, and rearing children is the ultimate communal action. The individual heritages of two people are joined in a unique new creation; all the physical, material, and psychic resources of both parents and of the larger community are needed. However, this communal social process of procreation and child-rearing has often been discussed in a misleading context. Labeling procreation as "rational," the "duty" of married people, is misleading both biologically and emotionally. Man's drive to reproduce himself may be less strong than the reproductive instinct in animals and less tied to mating, but it does exist. Distinctively human emotions reinforce the primitive drive for offspring.

* From *Beyond Birth Control: The Christian Experience of Sex,* Sheed and Ward, 1968.

Sensual delight in the physical presence of one's own child fuses with awe and delight in seeing the child's evolving mind and personality. Respect for individuality and personhood, wonder at the potential and development of human growth—these human responses give depth to the joy of peopling a uniquely created world of family and home. Parents create a continuously growing community wherein reciprocal love can be given and taken. Procreation is an instinctive pleasure, a joy, a delight, and a privilege—rather than a rational duty.

With divided man, however, every good drive is open to perversion. The drive for children is no exception. Children have been desired for all the wrong reasons, from self-aggrandizement and pride to revenge, economic security, economic gain. Freud suggested that one major psychic route to the desire for children was the sublimation of the early incest wish to have children by the beloved parent. This may well be a factor in development, but what is the source of this infantile irrational drive to procreate with the beloved parent? Man's mature sexual drive not only turns to beloved persons but becomes directed through desire and love to create and build future community. The "generativity" of Erikson's mature person most naturally comes to fruition through producing and rearing children. Despite the possible perversions, procreation joyfully fulfills man's individual and communal potential.

The writer of Genesis recognized the importance of procreation to man. Man holds his mandate from God to "increase and multiply and subdue the earth"; Abraham is promised descendants "numerous as the stars" as his reward for fidelity. This mandate and promise are not repeated in the New Testament, but the privilege, joy, and responsibility of procreation seem assumed. Christ tenderly accepted children, strongly affirmed their rights, and used images of child, childbearing, and family love in his teaching. His reference to the laboring woman's joy that a man has come into the world reveals his accord with the Jewish tradition. Conception, procreation, offspring—these are a blessing and privilege. Christ proclaimed as a portent of the horrors of the last times that the barren would rejoice in their barrenness. And it is only Christ's appreciation of family life that made him praise those who would leave all to follow him; only for the sake of the kingdom would family life be transcended. Even among the earliest Christians, who expected the kingdom to come so soon, childbearing and child-rearing are assumed to be the married's privileged service of God. Successful child-rearing allowed both women and men to qualify for leadership in the early Church.

Yet, as happened so often in the development of Christian thought, a priori assumption and joyful privilege became transformed into dutiful obligation when faced with challenge from heresy and an alien culture. Pagan license and Manichaean hatred of the flesh both denied man's procreative mandate, although for very different reasons. Moreover, the prevalence of infanticide and abortion elicited a Christian defense of innocent and defenseless life by emphasizing the duty to procreate and educate children in marriage. Finally, a revulsion at pagan selfishness and the influence of the Manichaeans coalesced and triumphed.

Suspicion of all sexuality grew to such proportions that eventually procreation became the only acceptable motivation for intercourse in marriage, or, worse still, child-rearing became "the price paid" for indulgence in the flesh. Yet, ironically, the suspicion of sexuality and the desire to defend celibacy and angelic marriages delayed any formal dogmatic statement of the couple's moral obligation to procreate. The primary purpose of marriage was defined as the procreation and education of children, and one could not frustrate conception; but until very recently the married could be praised for heroic sanctity if they lived in complete abstinence without producing children. However, such niceties of distinction, or so much abstinence, rarely prevailed at the popular level of Christian thought and practice.

Tainted married sexuality thus became totally bound and subordinate to procreation. The more children (and/or—however paradoxically—the more abstinence), the more holy the marriage. Applying all the celibate norms for an unmarried spirituality (negative norms at that) to the situation of the married resulted in much distortion. And the older forms of categorical thought and analysis misfired particularly in coping with the dynamic interwoven relationships of family life. Each act of intercourse was analyzed as a single isolated occurrence (as it would be for the nonmarried or in a static rational dissection), each conception and childbirth considered apart from the context of the existing family. An underground mystical stream of Christian tradition might include earthly love in a mystical affirmation of creation and God's dynamic love, but, generally, abstinence and rationality were the reigning ideals.

This inadequate Christian view of dutiful sexuality and procreation was encouraged by general conditions in the developing western culture. The necessity of marriage as a stable institution, combined with the fact of the low survival rate of both children and adults, placed all the emphasis on achieving fertility and building up the family. Gradually, however, with the growth of scientific knowledge and industrialization, the cultural situation changed and is changing still. No longer do most parents live in a society in which few survive childhood and where those who do prove to be an economic asset. Now, rather, it is anticipated that children will consume family resources instead of helping the family economy. There has been a revolution of child-rearing standards over the generations, with increased recognition of the requirements of time, attention, and education. The Christian west discovered childhood in the late fourteenth and fifteenth century as children emerged from "the anonymity in which their slender chance of survival had maintained them." Through raised expectations and educational demands, the pressures of successfully rearing a child have increased a hundredfold. At the same time, affluence and technology have been accompanied by certain breakdowns in stable community life. The individual couple, therefore, must meet greater economic, educational, moral, and psychological responsibilities to their children with less help. Children may never have been so enjoyed, valued, and understood, but this appreciation and understanding means that their need for family nurturing is seen more clearly. Those parents who are not exceptionally energetic and/or wealthy can also foresee that having more children may very well mean slighting the children they already have.

The technological revolution which created these new cultural conditions also produced new biological knowledge and consequent controls of sexuality and conception which challenge the old assumptions and methods of thought. Focusing on each sexual act in itself was more logical when the male semen was thought to contain the complete embryo, needing the female only for womb and blood. Female ovulation itself has been known for no longer than the age-span of the oldest members of our society. This one biological discovery radically changes our view of the nature of human fertility and sterility, and the implied norm of female sterility has not yet been fully considered. The increased life-span of modern woman insures that for two-thirds of her life she will be absolutely sterile (not counting the twenty-some sterile days each month during her childbearing years). Biologically, female sterility is more normative than fertility within the present life-span. Philosophically, therefore, individual acts of coitus cannot be as surely linked to conception when it is biologically known that repeated and continuous coitus is necessary to achieve conception within the varied and continuous human cycle of fertility and sterility. Moreover, with the further development of new hormonal controls of ovulation, a new dimension was added to the question of control. With "the pill," the growing challenge that widespread mechanical contraception had been giving to traditional Christian ideas became even more insistent.

The first moral problem that arose was the basic question of whether or not man should control his fertility at all. Should parents attempt to limit the number of children they would have? Intellectually and theologically, this had never been much of a problem; because the traditional option of marital abstinence, which would

in one aspect of the old view be an ideal marriage anyway, would inevitably limit children. In the first theological groupings with the problem of overfertility,
complete abstinence was given as the only acceptable
answer for a distressed couple. However, in popular de-
votion or "folk Catholicism" a view of providence prevailed which made even abstinence seem presumptuous.
God sent children to the married and God would provide for them; to control conception was to distrust
God's providence. The same nonreasoning superstition
that tolerated the medieval ordeal operated here; surely
an all-powerful God would not let the innocent drown
or the guilty burn, or, in the modern case, the newborn
starve. Secondary causes, rationality, and man's responsibility for the world were rejected as inconsistent with
true faith.

The new knowledge of the woman's fertile time of
the month was ignored, and the "rhythm method" was
generally rejected as less than fully Christian. In response to a group of French bishops, Rome ruled favor-
ably on a form of the rhythm method in the last century, but the inadequacy of the method's biological basis
kept the reluctant approval from spreading popularly.
In twentieth-century America a small group of deeply
motivated married couples enthusiastically embraced
a mystique of casting themselves upon providence in
their family life. Heroic sanctity was sought in marriage through having as many children as God sent and
living in the poverty and total generosity of the evangelical life. It is not surprising that this movement was
often accompanied by a back-to-the-land agrarianism
and a general rejection of technology. The rural mon-
astery with its unworldly and liturgical piety became

the ideal model for the home. The first generation of
these married laymen seeking perfection in their marriages and family life were excessive in their zeal (as
were the first desert hermits). And they were mistaken
in taking the contemplative or mendicant celibate
vocation as a model for marital sanctity. Casting one's
self upon providence is a different matter when you
will not bear the consequences alone. A child's welfare
cannot be sacrificed to his parents' search for sanctity.

The tendency to disregard the world and secondary
causes was gradually seen as a temptation to false su-
pernaturalism. Christ did not succumb to the temptation to ignore the law of gravity and cast himself from
the pinnacle of the temple to obtain supernatural intervention. Eventually, man's knowledge of the body and
the possibility of fertility control were seen as giving
moral responsibility to man. Man must choose once
he knows, for to knowingly ignore choice is a choice
in itself. A changing attitude toward the world encouraged new interpretations of Christian responsibility. The
realization that God made the world and gave it to man
to subdue modified the traditional tendency to passive
otherworldliness, and it could be seen that subduing the
world could include controlling the increase of human
beings. Logically, fertility control is as valid as death
control or pain control or any taming of natural forces
that man has achieved for the betterment of existing
human life. Man is distinctively human just because he
acts on himself and his world rather than being sub-
merged in nature. When Christianity can be understood
as a working-out of communal salvation, then a passive
acceptance of human fertility (or infertility, for that
matter) is not an adequate response.

For too long the awesome fact that a new child and immortal person comes into existence with each conception blinded man to the sad fact that in a disordered world the existing human beings in a family or a nation could be harmed by this new creation. Somehow, the fall of man which brought disorder to the world was not thought to apply to conceptions. An interesting analysis of the Genesis account of the fall, however, sees the punishment of Eve as including not only pain in childbirth but uncontrolled fertility in the "multiplying of conceptions." In point of fact, the disorder in our world reaches all the highest goods that man knows— life, marriage, work, procreation. Christians called to restore all things in Christ are called to correct disorder and to work toward harmony, the harmony of man with his body, his community, and his environment. Man can and should control procreation for a higher good.

This implication of the teaching of the Church became clear when the Second Vatican Council confirmed an idea of responsible parenthood. The council statement marked an acceptance and grasp of new realities by Christian authority. First, the Council recognized that the physical processes of nature have been so disordered that new pregnancies can be a real physical threat to the mother's health and life. This is a threat which she has a right to avoid for the sake of self-preservation. Secondly, the statement recognized that many social and psychological disorders are also beyond the control of the individual family and can make additional children a threat to the family's social health. Thirdly, a new recognition of social reality is matched by a new understanding of personal psychological re-

ality, i.e., the psychic dimension of sexuality which benefits the love and unity of married couples in themselves
and in their child-raising. In the Church's newest formulation, responsible Christian parenthood includes a
high evaluation of the sexual relationship of the parents.
Fertility control, therefore, must not damage the sexual
unity of the parents. But how? The means to fertility
control becomes the crucial theological question once
the right and responsibility of parents to control fertility
is granted. . . .

The testimony of Christian celibacy to the possibility
of full personhood and community without sexual fulfillment or progeny helped to modify the earlier pagan
and Jewish horror of sterility. When charity and unity
must extend beyond kinship or racial ties, then biologically producing family as family is not all-important;
building up the community becomes primary. Physical
nonparenthood implies no diminution of personhood.
The single, the widowed, the old, the child, the celibate
—all share in the kingdom according to their relationship to God. Women have not ended their useful life
after childbearing becomes physically impossible; female animals may not live beyond their reproductive
capacity, but people do. In humans sexual desire serves
the love and unity of the couple who must continue
growing in their love, as well perhaps as continue to
raise their younger children, long after further reproduction is impossible. Sterility is a natural occurrence
in the couple's life after the wife's menopause and even
at times during the earlier years of their marriage, as
when the wife is nursing a child. Only when kinship
groups are more important than general humanity does
sterility become a fearful fate.

Why, then, should artificial medical sterilization be

considered a forbidden mutilation of the person? Why has voluntary sterilization been so unacceptable as a form of control of conception? Of course, to sterilize without consent is a horrible violation of the individual person's rights over his body and its potential. When authority condones sterilization as a legal punishment and accepts legal judgment as to who is fit or unfit to procreate, then that society and its laws regress one step toward Nazi Germany. In the same way, when (as happened in the 1960's) an Italian theologian talks of the legitimacy of sterilizing the criminally insane, the Church moves back toward the Inquisition and the rack. The body is "for the Lord"; what we do to another we do to Christ. Those who countenance involuntary sterilization (or capital punishment) might well be shocked at the similar justifications for torture in Vietnam or Algeria. Can any community claim this much enforced right over any of its members? Christians, despite past guilt in assuming rights over another's body, must protest all forms of creeping totalitarianism which assume such a right.

Voluntary sterilization, on the other hand, is another matter. Essentially, voluntary sterilization in a woman does nothing more than quicken a natural and inevitable process of nature. Sterility is natural to a woman during most of her youth, and it is absolutely sure after a certain age. To end fertility for the good of the community, the immediate family, or the mother's health seems a rational function in subduing nature. Modern Christian moralists have never scrupled to approve Caesarian childbirth or the hurrying of childbirth by artificial means to insure the good of mother and child. Why should moral approval of earlier sterilization be such a different case? The Christian censure of sterilization has never been as strong as that against mechanical contraception, perhaps because of lack of knowledge or perhaps because of past lapses when the cutting off of a hand or other bodily mutilations were approved as punishments.

It is instructive to remember that in the recent controversy over transplanting organs the first reaction was to consider such removal of a healthy organ a forbidden mutilation. Finally, however, there arose an understanding that the principle of totality and intentional charity made the former definition of mutilation inadequate. The body has dignity and possesses a right to integrity, but not at the expense of the total organism. Christ himself spoke of laying down one's life for a friend and of casting out an eye in order to enter the kingdom of heaven. Cannot the potentiality of fertility likewise be voluntarily sacrificed to serve the greater whole? And is it not primarily the taboos and mystique that have surrounded sexuality—and made it "more sacred" than other potentialities—that have prevented acceptance of voluntary sterilization as a means of fertility control. Then too, in the past, procreation was considered a rational duty rather than a privileged right of human instinct and pleasure, and voluntary sterilization would be seen as social irresponsibility to the community. Now, however, the human species is no longer in danger of dying out, but rather in danger from the physical and psychological effects of overcrowding. In a country like India, suffering so desperately from overpopulation problems where famine decisively ends so many lives, should not—and even must not—man decisively end his own procreative potential for the good of others?

The sacrifice and decisive step of permanent sterilization would be foolish before a certain age and before procreative privileges in marriage had been exercised. But after a certain number of children and after a certain age, two married people should be able to accelerate the infertility which time will inevitably bring. The possibility of accidental death of one of the spouses or of children does not really present an objection; no loved person is replacable through procreation. Nor would such sterility limit love and service to the community; physical procreation is only one form of generosity. Naturally, voluntary permanent sterilization would never be an ideal, for no one relishes any permanent diminution of the body from baldness to toothlessness. However, sacrificing one capacity may better the whole in many situations.

To move to another specific case, the temporary sterility now easily achieved through chemical means has the very important advantage of being immediately reversible. Medically, oral contraceptives may yet prove to present dangers. Morally, however, as long as no new life is attacked, the totality principle again applies. The totality of the organism and the well-being of the family and community justify regulating fertility by increasing the time-span of the naturally occurring cycles of sterility. But first prohibitions of the moralists concerning the "pill" were based on extensions of the traditional reasoning and old assumptions. Primary and secondary ends of marriage were still distinguished, a distinction rejected, or at least ignored, by the Second Vatican Council.

In the first reactions to chemical contraception, as had been the case regarding mechanical contraception,

the old awed prejudice against sexuality was still reinforced by bad biological assumptions of the insepara-
bility of coitus and conception and the need to justify
the pleasure of sexuality by procreation. The basic assumption in which the old argument goes astray was
well stated in one of the current analyses of the problem: "All the traditional arguments against contraception imply this inviolable God-given direction to new
life in the sexual act and the sexual function; the difficulty is that they have not proved this, their major
premise." Why inviolable, why absolute? In the gospel,
sex is no more sacrosanct than other important faculties of man. Centuries of heresy and pagan influence,
however, created the taboo and mystique. And present-day conservatives, yielding to a reversal of thought
on the evil of sex, have ended up again with a view of
sex as "too good and too sacred" to be controlled by
man. Thus, those seeking a change in the Church's
teaching on contraception have been accused of giving
in to sexual license and/or desecrating the mystic I-thou
sacredness of the sexual relationship.

Misunderstandings and delays in the development of
a new morality result when new technology and knowledge have deprived the traditional natural law arguments
of a putative, static, stable order of nature to use as a
base. A recent elaborate philosophical reinterpretation
of the natural law argument assuming that procreation
for the married is a substantive good not to be actively
opposed founders on the primary assumption that procreation is still a substantive good in an overcrowded
world. The previous testimony of rational men to verify
this assumption means little, since all rational men at
one time or another have been misled. The past is not

the present, much less the future. Human nature does change, as radically as man's physique has changed over the centuries. Abstract philosophical arguments must be grounded in the present concrete human situation— and must realize, among other things, the limitations of human reason and the importance of human emotion.

Timing, context, and motivation give varied meanings to objective acts. A married couple fulfills their privilege and obligation in expanding their love and their community in a life together. Each act of intercourse need not be open to procreation—as, indeed, it could not be biologically. Only the misinformed understanding of the time sequence of conception can so identify coitus and conception that to intend one without the other is seen as irrational. Conception may even take place days after intercourse. Coitus also serves the unity of the couple, and often a couple will need to serve unity without at the same time expanding their community through procreation. Even if overcrowding and tension may eventually reduce human fertility naturally through evolution, those in need today cannot wait. In fact, the more expanded the couple's love and responsibility, the more the couple may need to be unified without having more children as the result.

All methods of birth control based upon extended abstinence err in a crucial and often cruel contradiction. Just when a couple's resources are overstrained so that having more children would be irresponsible, then the strengthening bond of sexual unity is also taken away by abstinence. Furthermore, those with emotional stability, economic resources, good health, and helpful friends and family will be able to cope with more children and so avoid prolonged abstinence. On the other hand, while those who are poor in emotional resources, material goods, or physical health are those who should limit procreation, abstinence for them may remove the one remaining, sustaining bond and resource of their marriage. Only the rich and insensitive can speak of any positive values in stifling what may be the one creative emotional expression and pleasure of those deprived of all other communication and community.

Moreover, the supposed self-discipline of prolonged voluntary abstinence is usually not helpful to the personality growth of the married. Illness, pregnancy, work, fatigue, and consideration for one's mate impose much necessary abstinence in which sexual desire is already sublimated. This discipline is inherent, necessary, and appropriate to the couple's life together, and is rather easily mastered by most mature loving people. However, when even more abstinence becomes the only means to avoid pregnancy, then abstinence can endanger the couple's unity. Even St. Paul warned that marital abstinence should not last too long, for fear of temptations to evil. The less strong are tempted to infidelity, solitary sexual fulfillment, or regression to more infantile satisfaction. The strong and independent who have worked hard to develop a unity in their common emotional bond are tempted to separate emotions and will and to overemphasize their independence. A little abstinence may be as refreshing and stimulating as silence is to speech, but too much suppression kills the desire for unity as the personality turns away from the source of frustration.

Complete abstinence in marriage can be all too easy after a certain amount of frustration. It is unfortunately true that "given sufficient motivation it is possible to reduce frustration by reducing erotic tension." But affectionate, independent, "friends," who can live in the same house without "erotic tension," do not encourage deep unity. Nor do they provide the proper climate in which to raise children well. Passionate parental love gives children a comforting sense of being transcended and excluded. "They don't live together just for me, so I don't have to live for them; I can grow up and make my own life." A strong erotic and romantic attachment of the parents to each other also provides the healthy, necessary frustration of the various infantile attachments which the child must outgrow to achieve psychic maturity. Moreover, sensing that his parents accept and share sensual sexual love helps a child accept his own sexuality and prepares him for his own marriage.

Children flourish in an aura of physical joy, relaxation, and openness. An atmosphere of uninhibited tenderness and delight in the flesh creates blooming infants, whereas the contrary atmosphere of family strain, irritability, repressed coolness and/or cerebral detachment withers a child. Also, it is well-known that when children are not played with tenderly, physically, and with delight, they become psychologically maimed and stunted (or even die). It is important that parents be open to expressions of joy and physical play with their children. At the same time, however, husband and wife must be so absorbed in their own relationship that the child is not subconsciously made into a substitute gratification.

In theory, the "rhythm method" of periodic abstinence would not create the tensions of complete abstinence. Control is effected through knowledge of the body's processes; the fertile time is ascertained, and abstinence provides an allowance of time so that sperm and egg cannot meet. In this method there is no irreversible and drastic change in the body, no chemically induced hormonal change, no spatial barrier to the male penetration, no interruption of coitus. Aesthetically and medically, rhythm far surpasses other methods of fertility control. When there is no interference in any bodily process, there can be no unfortunate side effects or disruption of functioning. And there is the happy absence of intrusive mechanical appliances or worrisome routines to be remembered.

Barriers of time are different from spatial barriers, contrary to one argument for contraception. The couple mutually effects this barrier, while a spatial barrier must be placed in or on one or another separate body and can be done without the knowledge or consent of the other. Only mutual decision about timing can control conception in the rhythm method. Control of the body through knowledge and will preserves a continuity and interested unity of man's psychic and physical potential. Margaret Mead felt that Samoan girls did not become pregnant during their affairs because of their ability to know instinctively their fertile times (like the promiscuous, primitive daughter who watched the moon in *Tobacco Road*). In voicing the hope that all birth control could be based on such a recovery of knowledge of the body, Margaret Mead expressed a very human preference for effective preventive knowledge rather than effective mechanical techniques. Father de Lestapis makes this same distinction between external "exogenous" techniques and the "endogenous" mastery of physiological functions of the organism. He also hopes much from future developments and research into the resources of the human body-mind synthesis.

However, it is just our present lack of sure knowledge of the physiological functioning of female ovulation that makes the rhythm method inadequate and often psychically destructive. The relatively short time of actual fertility cannot yet be predicted with certainty. Thus, an extended period of abstinence is now necessary to allow for uncertainty and/or variation in ovulation cycles. A short period of abstinence determined as biologically necessary for actual control of fertility could be easily integrated into a loving sexual relationship; minor obstacles increase desire and add piquancy. But an extended period of abstinence that requires serious repression with the necessary efforts of avoidance can engender all of the personal and family problems of permanent abstinence discussed above. Often, when cycles are short and/or irregular, and particularly when the need to control fertility is urgent, the periods of abstinence required will far exceed the supposed general norm.

But by far the worst burden of the whole method at this time is the anxiety caused by the lack of simple sure prediction. Even if all the efforts of calculation and constant preoccupation with physical measurements are viewed as a part of human responsibility and growth toward physical self-knowledge, the anxiety over calculation becomes destructive. Without the confirmation of medical or laboratory analysis, there can be little assurance that ovulation has occurred. While couples may try to duplicate a laboratory approach, they cannot live under sequestered laboratory conditions, especially when small children upset every routine. The emotional and physical vicissitudes of our hectic mobile lives often upset the woman's cycle. And the greater the strain on their emotional and physical resources, the less successful a couple may be at the rhythm method.

Worry over the correctness of calculation destroys the confidence and relaxation so necessary in sexual relationships. Conflict and tension often arise; for while each feels the imperative to show sexual love for the partner, yet each fears to impose the burden of another pregnancy on their marriage and family. The "double bind" of two opposing obligations can become torturous. As the reasons for spacing children or limiting children become more serious, then the psychic drawbacks of anxiety increase along with the periods of abstinence. Finally, when the conclusion is reached that no more chances can be taken with one's health and the good of the family, the only alternatives become complete abstinence or the use of an effective contraceptive. With all their aesthetic drawbacks, medical hazards, and canonical unacceptability, the effective contraceptives provide the best known control of fertility without sacrificing the normative sexual relationship of marriage. Values concerning persons far outweigh these difficulties; people come before things, the whole before the part. Those who claim that a woman employing a diaphragm shuts off her innermost self to her husband romantically overrate sexuality in life and ignore the total context of married sexuality.

Until the time when a technical breakthrough would make rhythm infallible without weeks of abstinence or anxious calculations of physical variables, many couples in good conscience will choose mechanical or chemical contraception. Chemical and mechanical contraceptives for the good of the marriage and family may be seen as a regrettable necessity in the same category as insulin injections for diabetics, hearing aids, false teeth, organ transplants, plastic surgery, blood transfusions, or any other intrusion or frustration of nature for the good of the total organism and community life. While sexuality is more intimate and important to the personality than some other functions of the person because of human subjectivity, the possible distortions, perversions, and personality failures present in sexual relations do not depend simply on reproductive "success." Can the defenders of the old tradition really maintain that the physical "mutilation" or "deformation" they attribute to the use of contraceptives (to use more pejorative words than "regulation" or "control") would be more immoral than the "shutting off," separation, and suppression involved in complete sexual abstinence? Is it not only the special fear-awe-sacred mystique surrounding sexuality that justifies sacrificing personal communication and pleasure to an abstract principle of a static natural law?

With the demythologization of sex, tolerance of the effective mechanical and chemical contraceptives (which, of course, do not attack new life) can be integrated in a new synthesis which incorporates the best of the old values with the best of new. Generosity, respect for creation and procreation, love for each other and for children need not be destroyed. Technology now provides an exogenous fertility control to families for whom no endogenous methods yet known can work. In the very near future new knowledge may make mechanical and/or chemical contraception as obsolete as a stagecoach compared to a jet plane, but looking to the future does not solve the present difficulties. Nor should worry over future depravities bar present concessions and change. Allowance of mechanical contraception and sterilization does not imply approval of perversion. The procreative mode of intercourse is still the sign of fulfillment of a couple's physical and psychic communion. The very psychic and social discoveries which first caused the reevaluation of sexuality and criticized the reigning rational biologism fully support heterosexual genitality as a necessary expression of maturity. Most psychologists might say something similar to Freud's comment on nongenital forms of intercourse; "they degrade the love-relationship of two human beings from being a serious matter to an otiose diversion, attended neither by risk nor by spiritual participation." Added to this testimony is the philosophical affirmation that the genital male-female giving and receiving in coitus is necessary as an aesthetic symbolic reality for the most complete expression of human love, mutuality, and communion. The biological rationale of the primacy of procreation is not the only bulwark against floods of moral and social chaos.

Fortunately, most Roman Catholic theologians who have reinvestigated and reexamined the question of birth control have been able to break out of the confining assumptions and fears which forbade all control of fertility other than abstinence. They have, of course, had to work through the taboo-mystique syndrome in which sexuality is feared and oversanctified. A new generation of Christian thinkers has struggled to a balanced view of sexuality which recognizes the importance of the totality of the individual organism and family as well as its consequent relationship to the adaptability,

survival, and betterment of the human race as a whole.
The new knowledge of the body and of evolutionary
theory has been accepted, and more and more of the
old biological misunderstandings are being exorcised.
Psychic and social reality has been given its due, along
with the importance of human cultures. As a result of
these theological reappraisals, the expert advice and
petition to Church authority has been to "change the
law," while the veiled and increasingly not-so-veiled
theological advice to the laity has been to follow their
Christian conscience if it leads them to use methods of
birth control other than rhythm.

Many of the laity have announced that their reason
and conscience enable them to reject past tradition and
teaching which has in their opinion been inadequate.
There is a definite division within the Church. The polls
reveal that many more of the silent laity have simply
begun using contraceptives and continued faithful at-
tendance at Mass. Others see continuing and widespread
doubt, apprehension, and general confusion as Catholics stumble about in the ruins of the *Romanità* synthesis. The birth control controversy is a symptom of
many more serious problems, and it inaugurates many
difficult decisions over control of lives. Objectively, the
birth control battle within the Church is an interesting
socio-religious phenomenon to observe, if rather complicated. One liberal assumption that progress and lay
initiative is always right breaks down when one re-
members those historical situations when the Church
began by giving way to lay, secular pressure and ended
by violating Christianity. The Inquisition, for instance,
conformed to lay wishes and current theories; the popes
of the time gave way, though only gradually; history

has recorded the result. On the other hand, the classic example of the Church's eventual repeal of its condemnation of usury comes immediately to mind. And no one can deny that in recent past centuries the Church has advocated Christian manifestations of social justice. But how often has this been only after gradually giving in and belatedly admitting the Christian basis of the reform? The Church, in these same recent past centuries, has failed slaves, women, democrats, workers, and Jews.

In the present birth control crisis, many members of the hierarchy seem well on the way to failing the married couple, the Christian family, and the underdeveloped countries with population problems. At the Second Vatican Council many bishops voiced dissatisfaction with the old tradition. It seems that no major theologians support the traditional view; and from the published reports, an overwhelming majority of the special commission advising the pope on contraception also recommend change. With such knowledge, educated Catholics can more easily follow their conscience and can speak with weary wit of the Papal teaching on birth control as "the pope's problem." But official governments, the poor, and those needing guidance cannot know or operate by inside information or subtle theological distinctions; they must depend upon the stated law and clear policy of the Church. For the benefit of those who, in the present situation of confusion and doubt, are not able to make a decision of conscience on the matter of contraception and who will never read or are unable to interpret the theologians, the hierarchy and Pope must change the ban on mechanical and oral contraceptives. . . .

Part II

5

Theologians' Statement [*]

———◆◆◆———

The following is the text of a statement by Catholic theologians disagreeing with Pope Paul's encyclical banning artificial birth control: Within two months over 600 Catholic theologians and philosophers had signed it.

As Roman Catholic theologians we respectfully acknowledge a distinct role of hierarchical magisterium (teaching authority) in the church of Christ. At the same time Christian tradition assigns theologians the special responsibility of evaluating and interpreting pronouncements of the magisterium in the light of the total theological data operative in each question or statement. We offer these initial comments on Pope Paul VI's encyclical on the regulation of birth.

[*] Published in, among other places, *The National Catholic Reporter*, for August 7, 1968, on information supplied by Father Daniel Maguire of The Catholic University of America.

The encyclical is not an infallible teaching. History shows that a number of statements of similar or even greater authoritative weight have subsequently been proven inadequate or even erroneous. Past authoritative statements on religious liberty, interest-taking, the right to silence, and the ends of marriage have all been corrected at a later date.

Many positive values concerning marriage are expressed in Paul VI's encyclical. However, we take exception to the ecclesiology implied and the methodology used by Paul VI in the writing and promulgation of the document: They are incompatible with the church's authentic self-awareness as expressed in and suggested by the acts of the Second Vatican Council itself. The encyclical consistently assumes that the church is identical with the hierarchical office. No real importance is afforded the witness of the life of the church in its totality: The special witness of many Catholic couples is neglected; it fails to acknowledge the witness of the separated Christian churches and ecclesial communities; it is insensitive to the witness of many men of good will; it pays insufficient attention to the ethical import of modern science.

Furthermore, the encyclical betrays a narrow and positivistic notion of papal authority, as illustrated by the rejection of the majority view presented by the commission established to consider the question, as well as by the rejection of the conclusions of a large part of the international Catholic theological community.

Likewise, we take exception to some of the specific ethical conclusions contained in the encyclical. They are based on an inadequate concept of natural law: The multiple forms of natural law theory are ignored and the fact that competent philosophers come to different conclusions on this very question is disregarded. Even the minority report of the papal commission noted grave difficulty in attempting to present conclusive proof of the immorality of artificial contraception based on natural law.

Other defects include: over-emphasis on the biological aspects of conjugal relations as ethically normative; undue stress on sexual acts and on the faculty of sex viewed in itself apart from the person and the couple; a static world-view which downplays the historical and evolutionary character of humanity in its finite existence, as described in Vatican II's *Pastoral Constitution on the Church in the Modern World;* unfounded assumptions about "the evil consequences of methods of artificial birth control"; indifference to Vatican II's assertion that prolonged sexual abstinence may cause "faithfulness to be imperiled and its quality of fruitfulness to be ruined"; an almost total disregard for the dignity of millions of human beings brought into the world without the slightest possibility of being fed and educated decently.

In actual fact, the encyclical demonstrates no development over the teaching of Pius XI's *Casti Connubii* whose conclusions have been called into question for grave and serious reasons. These reasons, given a muffled voice at Vatican II, have not been adequately handled by the mere repetition of past teaching.

It is common teaching in the church that Catholics may dissent from authoritative, non-infallible teachings of the magisterium when sufficient reasons for so doing exist.

Therefore, as Roman Catholic theologians, conscious

of our duty and our limitations, we conclude that spouses may responsibly decide according to their conscience that artificial contraception in some circumstances is permissible and indeed necessary to preserve and foster the values and sacredness of marriage.

It is our conviction also that true commitment to the mystery of Christ and the church requires a candid statement of mind at this time by all Catholic theologians.

6

The Right to Dissent[*]

◆◆◆

Gregory Baum

Pope Paul VI has made his decision. In the encyclical *Humanae Vitae* he condemns every form of artificial birth control, including the pill, as contrary to the order of nature and hence as an unqualified evil. He calls upon governments to refrain from promoting immoral practices among the people and asks Catholics to influence their governments in this direction.

That Pope Paul would decide to uphold the teaching of recent popes on this matter was a surprise and a shock to many Catholics and other people deeply concerned with morality and the future of society. The Pope's decision went against the majority report of his own study commission, against the almost unanimous voice of the Lay Congress held in Rome last year,

* From *Commonweal,* Aug. 23, 1968.

against the wishes of many bishops expressed at the recent meeting of the Synod, and against the weight of contemporary Catholic theology. The Pope rejected the Christian experience of vast number of Catholics and the witness of other Christian churches.

By what argument does Pope Paul establish his position? The argument, we note, is not drawn from divine revelation. The argument is based on rational reflection: It belongs to the order of reason. The fundamental principle invoked by the encyclical is the inseparable unity between love and fecundity in human sexuality. This principle belongs to the very structure of human life. It is a natural law. The encyclical makes this principle normative not only for the overall orientation of married life; it even applies it to the individual sexual act in marriage. Every sexual act, we are told, must be an expression of love and open to procreation. From this it follows that all mechanical means of birth control are against the order of nature. The same principle is applied to the use of the pill. The pill interferes with the natural, biological processes in man to render the marriage act sterile and hence must be regarded as against nature.

The reader of the encyclical familiar with contemporary Catholic theology may find that the argument moves too uncritically from the fundamental principle to particular applications. All Catholic theologians accept the inseparable unity between love and fecundity in human sexuality. This is basic to man's historical existence. In more recent theology this principle is applied to the total orientation of married life but not necessarily and under all circumstances to each individual sexual act in marriage. If a marriage is orientated toward love and

children in a general way, there may be circumstances
in which contraceptive birth regulation is permissible
and moral. It is quite widely held by theologians, even
by the more cautious, that since the pill does not interfere with the performance of the sexual act, its use is
morally indistinguishable from the rhythm method.

The Catholic people will not find the papal encyclical
easy to follow. It will be difficult for bishops and priests
to explain it to the people. It is difficult to explain how
a rule of life that is based on natural law and hence
corresponds to the universal moral experience of man,
is advocated in the present culture only by the Catholic
Church, unless one wanted to suggest that the consciences of other men and even other churches are so
corrupt that they are no longer in touch with the
foundation of human morality.

Bishops and priests will find it difficult to explain the
logic by which the encyclical moves from the general
principle to the particular applications. In particular the
word "natural" is used equivocally in the text. Natural
sometimes refers to what belongs to the basic structure
of human life. Here "nature" or man's fidelity to what
he is and is to be, is the norm of morality. To act
against "nature" in this profound sense is to damage
man's integrity. At other times the word natural refers
to biological processes in man. In explaining why the
use of the pill is wrong and why the rhythm method is
permissible, the encyclical says that the pill interferes
with the "natural" processes of human life while the
rhythm method does not. The use of the pill is, therefore, against nature and hence immoral. The word
natural is here used in two different senses. Priests will
find it difficult to explain to the faithful why something

that is against "nature" in a biological sense should necessarily be against "nature" in the profound sense of man's basic structure.

Many Catholics, bishops, priests and laity, have reflected on the issue for years. They have studied the writings of theologians, they have listened to the witness of Christians and men with sensitive consciences whom they admired, they have slowly formed their own conviction on the matter. Many Catholics have become convinced that birth control is not always against the nature of man. In many circumstances birth control is in accordance with man's historical nature to assume ever greater responsibility for himself and for his future. Man is summoned by God to assume responsibility for his history. What shall these Catholics do now? If they cannot accept the papal encyclical, must they leave the Catholic Church? We must examine this question.

The papal position on birth control is not an article of faith. It is not infallible. Papal infallibility has to do with teaching divine revelation. What does this mean? Papal infallibility has to do with what Jesus Christ taught us to believe and taught us to do (faith and morals). But the evaluation of birth control has to do with human wisdom. Many moral issues treated by the Church belong to this area of human and rational wisdom. (For instance, private property, religious liberty, the principle of subsidiarity, etc.) In this area the Church has the authority to teach, but here her teaching is always non-infallible and changeable. In other words, here the Church's authoritative teaching is fallible— which means that at times it can even be wrong. Catholics believe that since the ecclesiastical magisterium (teaching authority) is guided by the Spirit this will not happen very often. But there is nothing in Catholic dogma that assures them that it could not occasionally happen.

Since in the area of human wisdom and morality the Church teaches with authority, Catholics are always willing to learn and adopt the official teaching. They want to be docile to the teaching of bishops and popes. But what happens if they cannot assimilate the proposed teaching? What happens if this teaching goes counter to their own tested objective reasoning? Canonists and theologians have always held that under these conditions it is licit and moral for Catholics to disagree with an official position of the Church. In the language of the school books, the religious assent given to authoritative, non-infallible teaching is not absolute but conditional. When his convictions are based on tested and objective reasons, a loyal Catholic may rightfully dissent from the Church's official position.

The celebrated case here is the issue of religious liberty. When Catholic authors in the last century first proposed the separation of church and state as an ideal and advocated the principle of religious liberty, the papacy repeatedly condemned this position in encyclicals and other authoritative ecclesiastical documents. Many Catholics, including bishops, however, continued to hold to the principle of religious liberty. Deeply convinced of it, they disagreed with the official position. This happened especially in countries where Catholics lived in a pluralistic society and shared a new cultural experience as yet unknown and untried in Rome. Theologians continued to defend the principle of religious liberty. Eventually at Vatican Council II this principle, condemned in the last century, was fully acknowledged by the Catholic Church.

Catholics are not rebels in the Church. They love an ordered community. They acknowledge the authority of bishops and popes to teach, even in matters that go beyond divine revelation. But when their tested convictions demand it, they are free to dissent from an authoritative, non-infallible position of the Church. This freedom will be widely used by Catholics in regard to the papal encyclical. This freedom does not mean, of course, that people can do what they feel like. No moral person holds such a position. Life is always serious. A man must act according to his deep convictions about the meaning of human life. A man must follow his tested conscience.

Catholics who cannot accept the papal teaching on birth control need not leave the Catholic Church. Nor do they become hypocrites by staying in the Church. If they have formed deep convictions on the morality of birth control, they may dissent from the official position and follow their own tested conscience.

7

The Encyclical
Crisis *

————◆◆◆————

Bernard Häring

No papal teaching document has ever caused such an earthquake in the Church as the encyclical *Humanae Vitae*. Reactions around the world—in the Italian and American press, for example—are just as sharp as they were at the time of the *Syllabus of Errors* of Pius IX, perhaps even sharper. There is the difference, of course, that this time anti-Catholic feelings have been rarely expressed. The storm has broken over the heads of the curial advisors of the Pope and often of the Pope himself. The document is regarded as a great victory by those groups who opposed the Council from beginning to end. The conservative magazine *Triumph* is a typical example of the mentality of the far right: Of priests who do not believe what the encyclical declares, it

* From *Commonweal*, Sept. 6, 1968; portions omitted.

demands that they be honest and leave the Church since
they are automatically schismatics if they do not accept
the words of the Pope. The day after the encyclical
appeared, a doctor in consultation said: "Your Church
has lost two members; both of my Catholic colleagues
here have declared that they are leaving the Church,
since they find this whole mentality of the Pope unbe-
lievable." The same day a priest came with the question
whether he should not in honesty to his conscience give
up his priestly ministry; he could not act in accordance
with the encyclical. This traumatic experience, with the
great danger of a mass departure from the Church,
drove theologians to emphasize strongly the fallible
character of the encyclical and to take a courageous
stand.

If the Pope deserves admiration for the courage to
follow his conscience and to do the most unpopular
thing, all responsible men and women must show forth
similar honesty and courage of conscience. I am convinced that the subjective and conscious motive of the
Pope was love for the Church. Those who contradict
him must do it also out of love for the whole Church,
out of love for those whose faith is endangered. This
also can and must be a service of love for the successor
of St. Peter.

Monsignor Lambruschini, the Curia official appointed
by the Vatican to explain the encyclical to the press,
emphasized that it was not an infallible statement, and
that the possibility of a revised statement, if new data
appeared, could not be excluded. However, the tone of
the encyclical seems to leave little hope that this will
happen in Pope Paul's lifetime—little hope, that is,
unless the reaction of the whole Church immediately

makes him realize that he has chosen the wrong advisors and that the arguments which these men have recommended as highly suitable for modern thought are simply unacceptable.

Non-infallible but very authoritative statements of popes were in the past officially corrected only after a relatively long delay. Even when they were strongly criticized within the Church, this criticism became known only slowly. But the radical change which rapid communication has brought about in the modern world has created a totally new situation for authoritative Church statements, which are not infallible. The dialogue with the rest of the Church, which formerly took decades to unfold, takes place now in a matter of days or weeks. No significant theologian can write or express his opinion on an important issue without its being known almost the same day by anyone in the world with enough curiosity to learn about it.

In the past things were different. It took centuries before the extraordinarily dangerous "teaching" of the direct power of the pope over all temporal matters was rejected. It demanded courage for Friedrich von Spee finally to speak out openly and forcefully against the persecution, torture and burning of witches, a practice which had been recommended and doctrinally justified by a very authoritative encyclical of Innocent IV. For a long time the moralists did not dare to explain that the castration of the Vatican choir boys was immoral, since it had strong papal approval. The Council of Vienna explained in 1311 that theologians who tried in any way to justify usury were to be "imprisoned in iron chains" for the rest of their lives. And as late as the eighteenth-century, moral theology textbooks pub-

lished in Italy had to print that warning. Pius IX's
Syllabus lay undigested in the Church's stomach and in
her relationship to the world until the Second Vatican
Council's *Declaration on Religious Liberty* and *The
Constitution on the Church in the Modern World.* The
immorality of torture, which was justified for so many
centuries by the popes, and practiced in their name, was
condemned by a papal statement only after a long
period of time. Pius XII declared unequivocally that it
was against the natural law. The "Holy Inquisition"
and "holy wars" could have been wiped out from the
picture of the Church if the prophetic spirit and the
courage to speak out openly with Christian freedom
had been more highly valued in the Church. When the
popes and their curial theologians so frequently and so
emphatically defended temporal power and the Vatican
States as a divinely commissioned right and a spiritual
necessity, this critical Christian frankness should have
been more in evidence. Not only those who denied the
implications of "Thou art Peter," but precisely those
who believe in the spiritual mission of the office of
Peter must keep in mind the warning of the Lord
against an earthly conception of the Messiah: "Away
with you, Satan; you are a stumbling-block to me. You
think as men think, not as God thinks" (Matt. 16:23).

In discussing *Humanae Vitae* and the developments
of the last two years, the question, when all is said
and done, is really, "When you have come to yourself,
you must lend strength to your brothers" (Luke 22:31).
What is needed is an enlightened understanding of the
spiritual office of the successor of St. Peter, as it appeared so remarkably in Pope John, against the most
bitter opposition of that curial group which at the mo-

ment is triumphant, a group which, despite the era of
internationalization in which we live, was powerfully
strengthened at the last Consistory by the appointment
of twelve Italian cardinals. What is needed is the liberation for this ecumenical era of the papacy in the direction in which Pope Paul VI himself has already made
such giant strides. Call to mind the visit on two occasions of Paul to the Patriarch Athenagoras, before Paul
ventured to invite him to a visit in Rome. That was a
sensitive and delicate touch, a special sign of humility
of Paul with the Patriarch.

What is needed now is for all men in the Church to
speak out unequivocally and openly against these reactionary forces. This alone can prevent the reactionary
forces from pushing the Pope in the opposite direction,
back to that worldly narrowness exemplified in the
Syllabus and the Church prohibition of Italians from
voting in their own country which lasted from 1870 to
1929.

On the one hand the encyclical is quite optimistic
about the force of the arguments it proposes and the
information provided by the Pope's advisors, so that
"The magisterium could give adequate reply to the
expectation not only of the faithful, but also of world
opinion" (N.5). Nevertheless, when the Pope speaks
to "his own children" and to his "sons, the priests,"
optimism about the force of the arguments diminishes
somewhat. He asks for "loyal internal and external
obedience to the teaching authority of the Church" and
then adds: "That obedience, as you well know, obliges
not only because of the reason adduced, but rather because of the light of the Holy Spirit, which is given in
a particular way to the pastors of the Church in order

that they may illustrate the truth" (N.28). There can
be no doubt that our obedience of faith to the Church
rests on the confidence that the Church enjoys the
special assistance of the Holy Spirit in the explanation
of the Gospel and the guidance of the Church. But it
is not possible to make the Holy Spirit responsible for
everything which in past centuries was loudly asserted
in an authoritative tone by men of the Church. However, in *Humanae Vitae* the central argument is clearly
and unambiguously a thesis of the natural moral law,
and therefore a truth which is to be proven from human experiences and arguments of reason.

If the Holy Spirit gives a very special grace in the
composition and promulgation of this document, then
one may legitimately expect that this grace will manifest
itself in the way the question itself is handled. That
means in the solid presentation of proofs from human
experience and with good arguments. In my opinion,
that is not true in the present instance. Therefore, it is
no insult at all to the Holy Spirit if we continue to
express our doubts.

After the appeal to the Holy Spirit follows an exhor-
tation that for the sake of peace in the Church "all
should speak the same language" (N.28). This admoni-
tion is followed by the words of St. Paul (is this an
accurate translation?) that there should be no differences of opinion among Christians.

Paul opposed Peter to his face and expressed this
difference of opinion openly (Galatians 2), when Peter
had closed the doors to the spread of the Gospel, yielding in a moment of weakness to the pressure of the
Jerusalem curia. The theologians and bishops who now
raise their voices are not doing so out of *quarrelsome-*

ness but because if they do not, the credibility gap will be increased for the Catholic Church and many will find it impossible to belong to the Church because of the emphatic assertion of a constant human tradition in the Church. If, when all is said and done, the Pope abides unyieldingly to the conclusion of his encyclical, that in the Catholic Church only this one language of argumentation, mentality and commands may be spoken, then the voices of many men and women who love the Church must fall silent, and this one language will reach the ears of only a few, and not the ears of men with whom the future lies.

The argumentation of *Humanae Vitae* rests mainly on two points. The first is the constant teaching of the Church; the second is the absolute sacredness and inviolability of the biological functions in every use of marriage, so that every act must remain open for procreation, whether or not procreation can at this moment responsibly be undertaken.

Humanae Vitae differs from *Casti Connubii* by no longer making the effort to base the teaching of the Church in this matter on Genesis 38. It no longer tries to base its proof on Scripture. For every layman knows today that the intention of that text was to insist on the obligation to raise up children from the wife of one's dead brother, an obligation which is now forbidden by the Church. The text is not dealing with the absolute sacredness of the sperm.

So the only argument which remains is the fact that the Church has always taught this doctrine ("constant firmness by the teaching authority of the Church" N.6). In a chapter on tradition in one of my books I have attempted to show that the tradition is not so unequivocal as many think. Attention must also be given to the historical context in which the teaching was presented. But if the argument from tradition is to play so important a role, we must call to mind Jesus' struggle against the important role assigned to human traditions. "He also said to them, 'How well you set aside the commandment of God in order to maintain your tradition'" (Mark 7, 9). When the legalists asked the Lord "Why do your disciples break the old-established tradition?", Jesus answered "Why do you break God's commandment in the interest of your tradition?" (Matt. 15:24).

The encyclical must provide the opportunity for a better, more historically-oriented understanding of tradition and also of language. Think again of the insistence in Paul's creed that transsubstantiation is the most suitable word to express the real presence of Christ. This is to cling to words. Take as an illustration the English word "establishment". When I learned English, "establishment" was defined as "that which rests on a solid basis and therefore generates confidence." If someone in today's world wants to say that the Church rests on a solid basis and generates confidence by simply saying "The Church and the papacy is an 'establishment,'" then he has chosen the wrong word. Words must be understood in their context. Answers to the vital questions of a period are not magic formulas which can simply be "applied" over and over again.

The second argument is the biological understanding of the inviolable laws of nature. In the "hierarchy of values" (N.10), the biological seems to rate very high on the scale. The whole purpose of the act in its "metaphysical structure" is directed, so the argument goes, toward procreation and therefore every act must remain open to procreation, even in cases in which it would be absolutely meaningless and irresponsible to bring new life into being. "In relation to the biological processes, responsible parenthood means the knowledge and respect of their functions; human intellect discovers in the power of giving life biological laws which are a part of the human person" (N.10). I believe that biological functions are one part of man; but these biological functions are often upset; and the art of healing is possible only if man is a responsible steward of these functions and can intervene. It has not been proven that the biological functions connected with the power of procreation are absolutely untouchable and sacred, especially since they are often upset and, even according to the teaching of the Church, measures to restore health may be undertaken. The biological functions must be subordinated to the good of the whole person and marriage itself. This is, if I am not mistaken, by far the most common opinion in the Church.

Pope Paul's advisors hold to an absolutely biological understanding of the natural law. They have not even progressed from a very materialistic style of medicine to man-centered medicine, which views medicine not as the art of restoring biological functions, but of serving the whole person.

Pope Paul asserts that an intervention in the biological process necessarily destroys married love. This assertion has no more proof to back it up than the assertion of *Casti Connubii* that it is necessarly against the dignity of a woman for her to have some occupation outside the home.

The Second Vatican Council, following scientific developments in the field of moral theology, strongly de-

veloped the issue of responsible parenthood. There it is
clear that birth control is evaluated quite differently in
different circumstances. It is one thing if it is practiced
as the result of a conscientious decision that new life
cannot responsibly be brought into being here and now;
it is quite another if it is a simple rejection of the
parental vocation. Since Pope Paul makes the analysis
of the act his starting point, this fundamental distinction does not appear. The evil seems to consist exclusively, or at least principally in the violation of sacred
biological functions. The encyclical also fails to see that
abortion is a much greater problem than the methods
of birth control. In the encyclical, abortion is rejected
only in passing; the Council put its principal emphasis
on a condemnation of abortion. So the encyclical, from
a pedagogical standpoint, is rather confusing.

Pope Paul's encyclical gives an extraordinarily great
significance to the rhythm between fertile and infertile
periods. "God has wisely disposed natural laws and
rhythms of fecundity which, of themselves, cause a
separation in the succession of births" (N.11). Practically the only method permitted for responsible birth
control is periodic continence. "It is then licit to take
into account the natural rhythms immanent in the generative functions, for the use of marriage in the infecund periods only" (N.16).

Father Lestapis, S.J., and Father Martelet, S.J., who
are clearly among the superconsultors, have called the
rhythm between the fertile and infertile periods *"le
mystère sexual,"* the sexual secret of mystery. When I
asked, ironically, some years ago, "What happens when
the sexual mystery is not functioning properly?," without noticing the irony, the scholar answered "Then only
asceticism can help."

Here is the problem of the present teaching: Women whose periods are regular, who can use all the necessary means, including the possibility of an undisturbed temperature reading and, if necessary, seven doctors at their disposal, can live in accordance with the teaching of the Church. What about the poor, the uneducated, when their periods are irregular, or when, because of their level of culture, they are simply incapable of understanding these methods? What happens if these methods not only fail biologically, but lead to severe psychological disturbances?

Over the years I have received at least fifty letters which present cases in which the unsuccessful use of rhythm has led to psychoses for these women and required treatment for them in mental institutions. Just a week before the encyclical appeared, an English doctor wrote me that the confessor of a woman for whom he had prescribed the pill had refused her absolution when she had been released from a half-year of treatment in a mental institution after a pregnancy psychosis. And the superioress of an American hospital told me that the chaplain refused absolution to a severely ill woman who had taken the progesteron pill for the most valid reasons. He refused because she was not prepared to promise that she would take no more after her convalescence.

The encyclical *Humanae Vitae* is so apodictic and absolute that no exceptions of any kind may be permitted for objective reasons. The appeal for merciful consideration for the sinner can only be interpreted, it seems, to mean that one can be gentle only when one opposes the evil, that is, when the poor sinner has promised to amend.

In former years, even in the papal commission, I

Corinthians 7:1–5 was often cited. (". . . The husband
must give the wife what is due to her, and the wife must
give the husband his due. . . . Do not deny yourselves
to one another, except when you agree upon a temporary abstinence in order to devote yourselves to
prayer . . ." It is the only biblical text that has the least
connection with our problem. Paul warns energetically
against a long period of continence, since it can turn
out to the devil's advantage. This need not mean adultery. The devil has already gained a great deal if husband and wife are irritable and hostile. Psychologists
and concrete research, whose results were presented to
the Holy Father (from Mr. and Mrs. Crowley and
others) show that by far the majority of couples who
were questioned said that the practice of periodic continence over a long period had notably upset the
harmony of married life. All psychologists say also that
total abstinence from intercourse for a long period,
especially when forced on one of the partners, can be
very dangerous.

Relying on this psychological knowledge, and following Paul's line of thinking in I Corinthians 7, the Council gave this warning: "Where the intimacy of married
life is broken off, it is not rare for its faithfulness to be
imperiled and its quality of fruitfulness ruined. For
then the upbringing of the children and the courage to
accept new ones are both endangered" (*Constitution on
the Church in the Modern World,* N.51).

The failure of the encyclical to use either of these
texts is indeed one of its gravest defects. Here an un-
avoidable question must be answered by the theologians:
Can the encyclical *Humanae Vitae* be reconciled with
the teaching of Vatican II? This is a particularly acute

question for the present writer. In January of 1967 I received, by word of mouth, a very precise warning from the Holy Office (Cardinal Parente) because of what I had said in an interview for *La Rocca,* an Italian Catholic magazine. The remark which was found objectionable was my statement that the awaited statement of the Pope would obviously have to be based on the criteria which had been worked out in the Council document on the *Church in the Modern World,* and could not be a simple return to *Casti Connubii.* I was instructed that this was theologically incorrect: The Pope was not bound by the Council document. Later, for my further instruction, and warning, I received two memoranda *(monita)* of Vatican theologians: one of them said that the two documents, *Casti Connubii* and the Council document *(The Church in the Modern World)* could not be set in opposition to each other; it was simply a matter of one complementing the other. The other memorandum *(monitum)* instructed me that the doctrine in this matter was to be drawn from the encyclical *(Casti Connubii),* and that the Council Constitution was only "pastoral." This remark disregarded Pope John XXIII's opening speech of the Council in which he said that the teaching office of the Church was in its entirety pastoral.

In my opinion it is harder to reconcile *Humanae Vitae* with the Council Constitution on *The Church in the Modern World* than to reconcile the *Declaration on Religious Freedom* with the *Syllabus* of Pius IX, or at least no less difficult. This assertion is based especially on the fact (1) that the question just mentioned from the Council Constitution and the text of I Corinthians 7 are simply not taken seriously, (2) that the conception

of natural law of the whole pastoral Constitution of the
Council has simply not been incorporated into *Humanae Vitae,* and (3) that the criteria worked out in the
Constitution for the acceptability of methods of birth
control are not even mentioned and simply replaced by
biological "laws."

The question has been asked: does the encyclical bind
all Catholics in conscience? The Pope seems to answer
this question unambiguously. Nevertheless I believe that
one must give the Pope credit for not abrogating or
denying the general principles for forming a right conscience *(The Church in the Modern World,* N.16). My
answer along these lines is this:

(1) those who can accept the encyclical with an
honest conscience must do so, with all the consequences;

(2) those who doubt whether they can, must study it
thoroughly and also make use of further information
in order to form a clear conscience;

(3) those who, with an honest conscience, cannot accept the teaching and requirements of *Humanae Vitae,*
must follow their honest conscience. When married
couples, then, for good reasons and with a good conscience use methods of birth regulation which in their
minds are the most suitable—abortion is obviously excluded—they need not mention it in confession;

(4) Priests must instruct the faithful clearly about the
Pope's teaching. However, I do not see how they can
be denied the right to speak out their own opinion with
equal honesty.

The Pope did not follow that advice; he tried, with
the help of his close associates, to give reasons. Some
questions, of course, he simply did not put to himself,

perhaps with the intention of doing it at a later date. But it is really remarkable that in the long time they had, his advisors found no better reasons than those presented in the encyclical. The conclusion was settled. They had to find the premises to back it up. May others be more successful. But it seems that the conclusion doesn't stand very solidly.

However, what is most important at this time is that the authority of the Church not be destroyed. What must be destroyed is everything which is an obstacle to the reunion of Christians and spiritual leadership. When this situation has arrived, the Church as a whole and especially the Holy Father must find ways out of this impasse. More than that, they must come to a style of authority that can move effectively, inspire confidence and belief. The general direction must be toward collegiality and internationalization. But in this question collegiality must also be a sharing in the whole experience of the laity, especially of married couples and married counselors.

8

Frequent, Even Daily, Communion

◆◆◆

Michael Novak

How is it that Pope Paul VI and the writers of *Humanae Vitae* showed themselves incapable of understanding marital love? Nothing in that text suggests that the Pope or his advisors understand the argument in favor of contraception, let alone have adequate answers to it; nothing shows that they understand marital love. One reads their instruction respectfully, weighs it against one's own experience and one's own context, and then makes a decision. The Pope's word is but one of the words to be heard. It is not, on its own merits, a very perceptive or illuminating word. We have heard that word before, in fact, and have measured its inadequacy. Do the Pope or his advisors ever wonder why it is that men of good will, in good faith, do not see the matter as they do? Do they ever wonder why what seems obvious and good to them does not seem either obvious or good to others? How can there be such a large gap of misunderstanding between brothers?

The first assumption to make is that all parties to the argument are serious, of good will, and acting in good faith. Matters of life and death, of love and hate, are at stake; our lives are touched at the very center by this discussion. I am willing to assume that the Pope and his advisors, and men like Cardinal O'Boyle, are not perverse or malicious or acting out of duplicity. It is my temptation to think they are more concerned about the authority of the Church and about ecclesiastical consistency than about living human beings and the gospel of Christ. It is their temptation to think that those who oppose them are infected with secularism, subjectivism, or hedonism. If either side gives way to these temptations mutual understanding is impossible.

The second assumption is that neither group has a privileged access to "objective truth." The viewpoint of *Humanae Vitae* is, as nearly as the Pope and his advisors could determine, as close to the truth as they could arrive. But the viewpoint of those who defend marital contraception is also, in their considered view, as close to the truth as they can arrive. It is unlikely that both groups are totally in error, and yet at crucial points both views are in direct conflict. On these points, one of them is correct and one is incorrect; I do not accept an ultimate relativism. The first issue is to figure out why each side argues as it does—why serious men end in disagreement on such an important point. The second issue is to try to decide who is more correct, and which view better incorporates the truth of the other. I do not wish to try to answer that second problem; I wish to address myself to the first. How can it be that the Pope and his advisors take the view they do? It is a puzzle to me, for I find that view so alien and strange that I must work very hard to overcome the sensitivities and inclinations of intelligence developed over many years, in order to feel my way into their position. I can look at the world through their eyes only by the most strenuous effort of which I am capable. Correspondingly, I would feel more at ease if I felt that the Pope and his advisors would make the effort to look at the world through eyes unlike their own—if I felt that they truly understood what they reject.

Still, my main responsibility is for myself. And when I try to understand what I would have to change in myself in order to accept the viewpoint of *Humanae Vitae,* I find a whole series of presuppositions and attitudes that need to be brought into the light of day.

In the first place, there is a point of view suggested by the word "nature." In my present point of view, time is as much a dimension of nature as space is. I imagine nature to be a four-dimensional continuum. It is as "unnatural" and "artificial" to intervene temporally in this continuum as it is to intervene in it spatially. I do not understand why it is "unnatural" to block the spatial flow of the sperm so that it does not fertilize an ovum—to block it by diaphragm, or condom, say (however disagreeable such devices are)—and yet not "unnatural" to time the placement of the sperm so that it does not fertilize an ovum. In either case, human intelligence is directing the process so that the ovum will not be fertilized. In the first case, a physical spatial object is inserted in the process; in the second case, an equally physical temporal gap is deliberately (and with such care!) inserted in the process. I do not understand why spatial objects are blameworthy, while temporal gaps are not. Both are equally "natural" (or "unnatural").

Second, I do not understand why men who take aspirin, cold tablets, pills for ulcers, inoculations for small pox, and other assorted measures to "kill" or to modify the relations of certain juices, organisms, and cells in the body suddenly become alarmed when pills are taken to "kill" or to modify the relations of other juices, organisms, and cells. Is the ovum more sacred than the brain, the heart, the blood, the kidneys? Our whole lives are directed and shaped by the technical skills of modern medicine. Hence, when persons accept countless varieties of artificial intervention in connection with every other organism and cell, it is difficult to understand why suddenly their attitude changes when there is question of sperm or ovum.

In the same vein, it is difficult for me to understand why the Pope and his advisors do not recognize that it is as natural for a woman to be infertile as to be fertile. Why cannot human art enhance her infertility as well as her fertility? For infertility has its extremely important purposes as well as fertility does; a woman is, in fact, infertile for more days of the month than she is fertile. The act of intercourse is fertile only when a whole series of physiological conditions are in a certain configuration. Why is that configuration an especially privileged one, such that it provides a norm toward which all human art must be directed? Are not the other configurations equally natural? (They are, in any case, many times more frequent.) The Pope says all too easily, and without supporting physiological argument, that every act of intercourse is in itself directed toward procreation. That way of speaking is unsupported by either science or common experience, but is based on a concept which arose before the discovery of the cycles of infertility, and has in most circles been discarded since that discovery. Most acts of marital intercourse, plainly, do not result in procreation. There is no special reason to suppose that each act of intercourse was ever intended by the Creator to be directed toward procreation. Such a view seems to be a mere prejudice. It was a useful prejudice in times when the human race suffered from the threat of underpopulation and special reasons were needed to encourage large families. It is now a scientifically discredited prejudice, and a cruel and destructive one in practice, both for overpopulated regions of the earth and for fearfully strained families in advanced, industrial nations.

Third, it is difficult to understand why the Pope and his advisors have no insight into the destructiveness of fear and uncertainty upon young mothers in industrial societies, whose duties include far more than being the casual mothers of large rural families. In the economics of the large modern city, planning is the only route to survival, health, responsibility; it is immoral and irresponsible to bring new children into many situations. Women are entitled to all the possibilities of humanistic development formerly open only to men; the riches of western civilization are theirs, too. They, like men, need to plan their own careers, to devote time to study and to work at a profession, to continue a steady program of intellectual or other professional training. Their children benefit from such development on the part of the mother, both because the mother is then not so tempted to "sacrifice herself for her children" in a psychologically destructive way, and because the mother's richer human development teaches the child, too, the value of freedom, discipline, and development. When she is uncertain which acts of lovemaking will dramatically alter her life for the next several years, a woman makes love with fear, uncertainty, resentment, and depression, not with joy and affection. The Pope and his advisors show no awareness whatever of a feminine point of view.

Fourth, it is easy to understand that children are a major good of marriage, and that married couples have a moral invitation, if not obligation, to have children. But a healthy couple can have as many as twenty or thirty children in the normal course of marriage, if they care to. Given the diagnostic techniques of modern medicine, it is relatively easy to have as many children as a couple desires. One could, for example, decide to have twelve children and—with a little bit of luck—succeed in doing so with twelve precise acts of intercourse during the whole of one's married life. Is it some sort of moral idea to have as few acts of intercourse as possible? It is difficult to understand why intercourse is to be treated in a different category from eating, drinking, sleeping, and other similar human activities—all of which are not merely physical but specifically human, symbolic, and communitarian. Why should not married couples be urged to have intercourse every day, or even more often if they can? The juices and movements of the human body have their own rhythms; why should they not be followed by drawing them into a whole human context of sharing and joy? It is good to eat and drink. It is good to make love. Why not eat, drink, and make love daily?

Fifth, it is easy to understand that intercourse seems to be mere indulgence, selfishness, and lack of self-control to celibate persons who are striving hard to remain celibate. Their self-denial must lead them to imagine that intercourse is release, loss of self-control, softness, animality. Many married persons, too, have been taught by celibates to think of intercourse in that fashion. They are slightly ashamed to find themselves making love. To them, it seems like giving in to an animal instinct. "Why, if it were not for the prohibition against contraceptives," more than one Catholic woman has been heard to say, "we would be like mere animals." How sorry one feels for a woman's husband and for her, if love-making is in her mind a nasty, short and brutish business, justified only by the having of children. What terrors and ugliness her psyche must undergo, during love-making so accepted! One wonders what can have led human beings to have nullified the tenderness, playfulness, and restorative powers of love-making, and to have turned a joy of body and spirit into an exercise in bestiality.

For love-making is an act of the human person, of intelligence and sensitivity, of gentleness and respect for one another, of struggle and of happy combat. The whole psyche is involved in it: one's skin, one's emotions, one's juices, one's mind, one's perceptions, one's freedom, one's aspirations. Animals have babies, but they do not make love. Human beings create an art of playfulness and make love, not when they need to, but when they wish. It is those who make love only in order to have children who mechanize and dehumanize the act of intercourse.

Sixth, I have never understood why there is anything especially sacred about male sperm. It is plentiful and a bodily juice like many others. For many men, the more they use it the more plentiful it becomes. There is no need, then, to venerate it. (Only last week I heard a Catholic college junior speak of spilt sperm as "the

murder of a possible child." Recalling the role of
women, the least he could have said is "the murder of
half the possibility of a child." Incredible notion!) The
manifestations of masculine narcissism are devious beyond tracing; not least in a celibate culture. Most persons today would be embarrassed to take the veneration
of male sperm seriously enough to argue against it; but
the idea persists. It provides the image of contraception
as an act of "malicious interference with intent to kill";
the sperm is imagined as a living being, a possible human being. It is reverenced as the vessel of life. It is
not treated as an ordinary bodily fluid like all the
others.

Seventh, those who think contraception is evil seem
to have an inexperienced and lamentably deficient image
of the uses of intercourse. To assume that image, many
married couples would have to alter their entire experience. The root of the difficulty is that the Pope and his
advisors assume that theirs is the moral view of intercourse; whereas it seems that their view is gravely inadequate, and even immoral. It is immoral not only
in the larger sense that they fail to address the overwhelming problem of overpopulation. It is immoral in
the more intimate sense that they fail to understand the
occasions, the feel, the significance, the moral value of
intercourse. When they speak of marital intercourse,
they try to speak of a beautiful ideal; but their ideal is
in fact out of touch and, in the end, morally ugly. They
seem to imagine that intercourse is an animal act, a
selfish act and often an act of lust, a loss of self-control,
a demeaning of one's humanity, a giving way before indispensable but shameful instincts, an act of efficiency
redeemed only by the possible production of children.

They seem to want the fewest number of acts of intercourse possible; whereas it seems both more human and more Christian to encourage couples to make love as often as possible. They seem to want each act of intercourse to carry the risk of childbirth; whereas it seems both more human and more Christian for couples to seek to have children at precisely those times when their sense of responsibility instructs them it is prudent. The repercussions of having a child are too important to entrust to chance; and to depend upon Providence in matters that depend upon ourselves is not at all praiseworthy.

Thus, finally, the argument between the Pope's theologians and those theologians who defend contraception is not between the former's morality and the latter's immorality, but between opposite views of what is moral. What the Pope proposes as moral seems to many of us immoral; and what he calls immoral seems to us more moral by far than his own views. To have children is, for most couples, easy; and apart from those two or three or four or five times in their life when having intercourse is to result in having children, intercourse is their joy, sustenance, and precious instructor in understanding and love. It is not easy to arrange to have intercourse. Children keep the house in confusion; daily occupations fill the mind, drain the emotions, and eat up the hours of the day and evening. At night, one or the other partner is sometimes tired; the other may be away or busy at work. The routine of marriage makes passion quiescent. Unless the partners positively strive to arouse desire and responsiveness, they can easily drift into a sort of mechanized, pragmatic partnership. It is extremely important for them to create occasions for lovemaking, and to develop their physical warmth and responsiveness. The desire for lovemaking is not automatic; it needs cultivation, the more so in proportion as the daily schedule is heavy. There is a danger in modern households that lovemaking will become pale and routinized, unsatisfactory and finally abandoned altogether. And when lovemaking dies, something most precious in the development of the couple dies.

For contraceptive lovemaking teaches gentleness, alertness, responsiveness, patience, humor. It operates as a measure and criterion of full and perfect love. For as a symbol it says more adequately than words can that the two are one. The resistance and reluctance that one or the other partner sometimes feels instructs them that something is injuring their oneness; it suggests hidden resentments, fears, complaints; it forces the lack of unity out in the open. Moreover, lovemaking in its intimacy prompts a couple to do what modern couples seldom have time to do: talk. It provides quiet hours of conversation, of shared griefs and successes, the sadnesses of partings and the overflowing joy of return. It knits the emotions, feelings, and instincts of the couple together. It does not allow them to live together like college roommates or mere chums; it introduces them to a wholly different—and infinite—dimension of intimacy. It liberates both wives and husbands in a competitive society from the atmosphere of fear, efficiency, and productivity; it allows them to play, with spontaneity, in an act of love that is an end in itself. It prevents them from becoming indifferent to one another, from succumbing to routine, and from merely taking one another for granted. It obliges them to try to penetrate

through to the secret and hidden recesses of one another's passions, fears, and hesitations; it leads them to
unsuspected capacities for joy, excitement, and arousal.
It makes them feel that they are still young, alive, and
full of love.

For all these reasons, frequent intercourse is a moral
imperative. It would be nice if there were no ants at
picnics, no need for impeding clothes to protect us from
rain, no usefulness in inoculations and pills against diseases. Pure spontaneity without technique would be like
innocent childhood. But at every important point in
human life, human art is called upon to enhance nature,
to liberate it, and to lead it to its highest fulfillment.
Children are lovely and, in their own right, a very
special joy. But even when children are not in question,
lovemaking has an indispensable and important role in
marriage. It is as natural for sperm not to meet ovum
as to meet it, and human art is appropriately applied
to either goal: lovemaking in and for itself, or love-
making with the additional purpose of having children.

I wish, as a minimum, that the Pope and his advisors
could show some understanding of this and other points
of view. But my long-term hope is that one day the
Catholic Church will support the idea of contraceptive
love-making in marriage, not grudgingly, but with the
enthusiasm that arises from perceiving clearly the power
of love and joy that flow from frequent, even daily,
marital communion.

9

Have You Thought
It Out All the Way?

◆◆◆

Mary Perkins Ryan
John Julian Ryan

At first sight, the chain reaction caused by the publication of *Humanae Vitae* seems quite out of proportion to the cause. Why should the Catholic Church—in so many of its members and structures—be so shaken by a concern not easily seen as connected with the central message of the gospel? One reason seems increasingly clear: that the Church's age-old position on contraception is the result of many other attitudes and positions, basically philosophical or cultural rather than evangelic, which the "teaching Church" has taken on in the course of the centuries. In the context of these positions, a complete ban on contraception made sense. But, during the last decades, creative theologians and the lived experience of a growing number of thoughtful Catholics have been moving toward other positions, forming a new context in which the problem of contraception appears in a completely different light.

The present anguishing situation arises from the fact that *Humanae Vitae* was written out of the old context —which no longer makes sense to a considerable proportion of the Catholic community. People who see things in the new way cannot go back to the old one and may, consequently, if they are priests or teachers, become involved in many difficult confrontations with Church authorities. But far unhappier is the situation of the many couples who have been using "the pill" or some other means of contraception while still thinking in the old context. They had been using it, or had been advised to use it, on the grounds that the question was now an open one and therefore they could follow their consciences. If Pope Paul had accepted the majority report of the papal commission, or even sanctioned only the use of "the pill" as a "natural" means of birth prevention, then all these people could have gone on doing what they were doing with a clear conscience, and a great many more would have joined them.

But now, with the publication of *Humanae Vitae,* the whole question of "following one's conscience" is raised afresh. Innumerable people are now disturbed; and priests who believed that they had helped many couples to realize their right and duty to follow their consciences in this matter are now dismayed to find them back where they started from.

The reason, it seems to us, is that such people never had the need or opportunity really to think through the implications for a Christian of "following one's conscience." A priest or other advisor had told them that they would not be committing mortal sin if they did what they seriously thought best for their marriage and their family in this particular matter, and they followed his advice. But they did not ask themselves the basic questions: What is moral behavior for, anyway? What does it essentially consist in? How does one form one's conscience as to what is or is not moral behavior? What is the role of Christian tradition, and of the Pope and bishops, in this process of forming a Christian conscience? How does one go about deciding in the concrete what is the right course of action?

Consequently, now that the Pope has spoken, a great many Catholics who are convinced that they must use contraceptives feel that they must leave the Church. Others feel that they should consider themselves Catholics in a state of mortal sin, unable to receive the sacraments. And a great many more, whether or not contraception is their personal problem, feel that this statement of the Pope's is the last straw; they can no longer find the Church credible.

It will be a tragedy if any sincere Catholic feels forced to leave the Church because he cannot agree with the Pope on this matter. We who disagree with him are "the Church" too; we are all members of one another and we all need each other. It will be an equal tragedy if married Catholics feel that they are committing mortal sins in a use of contraceptives that they feel essential to their marriage lives and therefore cannot receive the sacraments. Today, more than ever, we need the whole community of the Church celebrating the eucharist in unity. And it will be a tragedy for Catholic couples to continue to jeopardize their marriages, their health, or the welfare of their existing children and their society in "blind" obedience to the Pope's teaching, or because the development of birth control programs has been slowed down because of this teaching.

On the other hand, if the present unhappy situation causes more Catholics to think out, discuss together, and put into practice what is involved for a Christian in "following one's conscience," then the radical renewal of the Church may become a real possibility. For this renewal ultimately depends on whether a significant number of Catholics abandon the "pay, pray, and obey" mentality too characteristic of the past, and take on one of Christian responsibility.

We are therefore here attempting to present an overview of the various attitudes or positions on sexual morality, on morality and on the mission of the Church involved in the traditional teaching about contraception, and also of the directions in which Catholic thinking and experience have grown, or are growing, away from them. This overview will necessarily be an oversimplified and summary one. Quantities of literature exist on each of its elements and aspects. But we hope that bringing together these issues in a fairly compact form will clarify the very vital fact of their interdependence, and will also encourage readers to further thought, study and discussion.

"Man is a creature composed of body and soul," but he would be much better off without the body. This is certainly not official Catholic teaching, but it is equally certainly the impression given by much of the religious education of the past, by "spiritual" literature, and even by some liturgical texts. Through his body, man is tied down to the material universe and material cares, whereas his true home is in a spiritual realm unfettered by matter. Still more, attending to the physical necessities of his body and its urges at best distracts him from higher concerns and, more likely, leads him into sin. In order to become truly human and holy, we must therefore repress our concupiscible and irascible urges (passions) as thoroughly and consistently as possible. If we can come to ignore them completely, so much the better. To become more and more "spiritual," in the sense of less and less concerned with material and temporal realities, is the ideal, but the ordinary Christian must at least try to "so go through the things of time as not to lose those of eternity."

The worst element of these unfortunate bodies of ours is the sexual, because our sexual urges are so strong, so hard to control by reason and will, and so prone to lead us down from higher things to wallowing in the sensual and material. Because the exercise of our sexuality almost inevitably overwhelms our higher nature, any sexual pleasure deliberately indulged in outside of marriage, or illicitly in marriage, is mortally sinful, and even its lawful exercise in marriage can hardly help being at least venially sinful. Besides, it is through intercourse that original sin is transmitted from generation to generation.

On the other hand, God wants more souls enjoying the happiness of heaven, and he therefore commanded man to "increase and multiply," and sanctioned the institution of marriage as the only proper context for this increase. Consequently, while the state of celibacy or virginity is far higher than that of marriage, it is not sinful for Christians to marry. But since the only really legitimate reason for marrying is to produce and bring up children, the only legitimate reason for having intercourse is procreation. Again, every human life is sacred because God infuses an immortal soul into the body procreated by the parents. Consequently, abortion is clearly the equivalent of murder. But also, since the male seed is the active principle in the generation of new human beings, it, too, is sacred, and willingly to deposit it anywhere but in the vagina of a woman in order to produce a child is hardly distinguishable from abortion.

The only reason for God's having created women would seem to be that they are necessary for the procreation of children; since in every way they are inferior to men. Unfortunately, women inevitably tend to arouse men's sexual urges and lead them into sin. Was it not Eve who led Adam to fall? It is therefore better to keep men and women apart as much as possible, except in marriage.

To complicate human life further, some men and women consider what attracts them to one another to be "love." But this kind of love is not really worthy of the name, for it is inevitably a desirous and selfish love, seeking something for itself—whether this something is simply the pleasure of enjoying the other's body or some supposedly more "spiritual" kind of union with the other. In fact, even the love of friendship involves some *quid pro quo* and is always prone to take on a latent or overt tone of sexuality, even between members of the same sex, and so may very easily lead to sin. Human love is, then, generally suspect, except possibly the love of parents for their children. The only form of love the Christian should try to cultivate is the completely generous self-giving love that seeks only the good of the other, the love proper to God himself, the love that he gives us as one of the theological virtues: "charity" or *"agape."*

The only hopeful elements in this dismal picture of human nature, human sexuality and love are, obviously, the ideals of respect for the individual human life, however weak and unimportant, and the ideal of self-giving love. These are the peculiarly scriptural and Christian ideas in this complex; the rest are drawn from religio-philosophical notions and cultural assumptions current in the Graeco-Roman world in which the Church began its existence, which have been influential both in society and the Church in one or another form, through the centuries until our own time.

Moreover, the Church never officially endorsed the view of matter or the human body as essentially evil; the doctrines of creation and of the resurrection of the body and the renewal of all creation have always been proclaimed against this view. Again, the Church has always upheld and tried to strengthen the institution of marriage: even St. Augustine, who is so much blamed for the lasting innfluence of his gloomy views about human sexuality, included "faithfulness" and "the sacrament" as well as "offspring" among the "goods" of marriage. Many more positive strains in Christian thinking developed through the ages in contrast to these negative notions (see John T. Noonan, *Contraception,* Harvard University Press, 1965, for a scholarly but readable history). And, surely, the common sense of Christian people and the vital force of the Gospel have enabled innumerable Christians to live and love in a more hopeful and human fashion than the above assumptions would indicate.

But we have all been formed by these ideas to a greater or lesser extent, both as members of our society and as Catholics. A vast and growing literature about today's "Sexual Wilderness," (the title of Vance Packard's recent book) and what might be done to humanize it, testifies to the current struggle to sift out the perennial values and norms contained in our complex and contradictory collection of inherited socio-sexual attitudes and mores, and to foster these values and norms in ways consonant with today's new insights and conditions. We Catholics cannot help taking part, passively or actively, in this struggle.

As Catholics, we have perhaps been more explicitly influenced by some of the pessimistic attitudes sketched out above through the teaching in not-too-old texts about "bad" parts of the body, the high priority given to celibacy and virginity in the Church, the second-class position of women in the Church, the regulations of many seminaries and religious orders, all of which have been handed on to students taught by these priests about the dangers of "particular friendships," etc. Certainly, during the last decades efforts have been made in the Church to work away from what is humanly degrading and opposed to the spirit of the gospel in the ideas and attitudes just sketched out. In particular, the Council's *Constitution on the Church in the Modern World* contains a fine expression of the ideal of married love and the "noble and worthy" character of the marital act. By now most of us are probably intellectually convinced of the falsity of our inherited distrust of our bodies, or our sexuality, and of human love; and of the falsity of many existing stereotypes about men and women and the relationships between them.

But most of us need to make a conscious and persistent effort to work towards the more positive and balanced ideas and attitudes opened out by modern developments in theology, philosophy and the social sciences, in the context of today's situation.[1] Some of the key elements we have to work with are:

(1) The biblical idea of man as a *body-spirit* entity, a psycho-physical whole. We do not merely "have" our bodies; we *are* our bodies. Some modern philosophers have been developing a very important implication of this view of man: that our bodies are our primary mode of presence to others; human relationships would be impossible without our bodies. Another implication is that we are masculine or feminine *persons;* our sexuality is inseparable from our way-of-being-with-others, but our personality is primary.

(2) The biblical usage of the terms "flesh" and "spirit," as in St. Paul's dichotomy between "the life of the flesh" and "the life of the spirit." This does not mean physical life, sensual life, as opposed to the life of the mind or soul. The "life of the flesh" is the life of the whole human person in the state of ambiguity, weakness, incompleteness, liability to alienation, frustration, pain, death—in other words, what is often called today "the human condition." "The life of the spirit," on the other hand, is equally the life of the whole human person, but fully alive in himself and in his relationship to his fellow men and God, human life as God means it to be, the life of which the risen Christ is the exemplar.[2]

(3) An ideal of mature human love at which we can

all aim in our daily lives and in all our relationships, developed by philosophers such as Martin Buber and psychologists such as Erik Fromm and Carl Rogers. This love is respectful of the other, open to the other, deals with the other as a person and does not use him or her as a thing; it is generously self-giving for the other's good and open to receive the other's self-giving. This is how we should try to love everyone, and this is the mode of loving that should gradually inform and direct our affective drive and its sexual components. In other words, we should try to love in this way when we are loving affectionately and passionately as well as when we are trying to "do good" to people whom we do not like.

Now, this picture of mature love very closely corresponds to the New Testament's picture of the way Jesus loved in his various relationships with other people and with the characteristics of love given by St. Paul and St. John. If we really believe that "where charity and love are, there is God," we must believe that God is present wherever people are trying to love one another generously, maturely, "in deed and in truth."

An essential characteristic of mature love—whether as described in modern or New Testament terms—is that it is creative, life-giving. This is true in many senses. To go out of ourselves in love makes us truly alive: "We know that we have passed from death to life because we love the brethren," and all of us have experienced in loving some sense of new freedom and vitality. Equally, human persons cannot survive and grow up healthily without being loved. Small babies need "tender, loving care" as well as attention to their physical needs or they will sicken and die. Children need strong supporting love to go through the crises of childhood and adolescence healthily, to be able to venture to grow up, to learn how to love. (As Rabbi Heschel says, we have to be able to *respond* to others and to God, before we can become *responsible*.) The same thing is true, in many degrees and ways, of all of us all throughout our lives; we need to be loved to become our best selves. And, obviously, love is creative through the actions it motivates: healing, reconciling, feeding the hungry, changing unjust social conditions, peacemaking . . .

Mature love, then, is never an *"égöisme à deux."* It must be radiating and creative, or it is not real love. The paradigm of love's creativity is, of course, the marital love which gives birth to children and brings them up lovingly. But this is not the only kind of creativity possible to married love; husband and wife can be a focus of loving concern and action in their community and their society; their love for one another can make each more creative and effective. To say, then, that married love cannot be life-giving and creative when it is not producing children it to take a very narrow and biological view of both love and life.

(4) An optimistic view of human nature as basically tending to be outgoing, open, loving, creative and becoming self-centered, closed, hostile, alienated mainly because of the various threats posed to the person by his total environment. Such a view is not opposed to that of St. Thomas who held that human nature was "wounded" but not "corrupted" by the fall, as did the Catholic view stated by the Council of Trent in opposition to some of the Reformers. And some theologians today are suggesting that the negative influences in any human environment—compounded from cen-

tury to century and affecting to some extent even the genes and chromosomes that will form the next generation—are what is meant by "original sin" in present-day terms.

To adopt this view does not mean that one takes an unrealistic rosy view of oneself or other people or the human condition. But it does mean that one has hope in one's own potentialities and those of others, in the spirit of love at work in people. It means that one tries to be loving, to awaken and strengthen other people's capacities to love. It means that one goes to work to try and change evil conditions and structures conducive to producing "evil" people.

To summarize: The "old" complex of mainly pessimistic attitudes about human nature, the body, sexuality, and warm or passionate love flows from the conviction of a basic opposition between body and soul, matter and spirit. To locate the ambiguity of the human situation here is unscriptural and essentially non-Christian. It should be located in the opposition between love and life (seen as inseparable) on the one hand, and hatred, alienation, and death, on the other. God is love. God is life. God is on the side of love and life. To become more loving and, consequently, more life-giving is to become more "spiritual," to become more like God. This is why he sent his Son: to show us how to love, to enable us to love and so to live.

To the "old" complex of attitudes, which, even with its pessimism, includes the Christian reverence for human life, contraception inevitably appears to be "intrinsically evil" for it seems to involve at once giving way to the worst element in man and preventing this element from achieving its only legitimizing purpose, the procreation of a child. The "newer" complex of attitudes oriented toward fostering mature and loving human persons ("spiritual" persons in the proper sense) seems to offer no grounds for believing contraception to be "intrinsically evil." Under certain conditions, carried out for loving reasons, it might be positively good.

Most of us probably grew up with a general notion that human actions are right or wrong because God said so (through the medium of our parents and the Church). Many of us were surprised to discover—it happened to us through reading F. J. Sheed's *Map of Life*—that the Ten Commandments and their explication by the Church are not arbitrary rulings but "Maker's instructions." They are to be obeyed because they show people how human nature works best; to disobey them is to harm oneself and others, just as the car owner will ruin his car if he doesn't do what the manual prescribes.

However, the car owner who damages his car through disobeying the maker's instructions may feel remorse at his own stupidity or carelessness, but he does not feel moral guilt, unless—like many New Englanders—he was brought up in an ethos in which carelessness and treating things irresponsibly were felt to be immoral. For, as psychologists agree, the origin of our feeling guilty about this or that action lies in the prerational, childhood fear of losing our parent's love and care if we displeased them.

This fear of losing our parents' love was for many Christians, through their parents' words and attitudes and religious instruction, developed into a fear of (also) losing God's love by disobeying his commands and wishes—of losing his love and so going to hell. And, as most of us grew up, we learned in more and more detail (especially if we received regular religious in-

struction via the Baltimore Catechism or one of its de-
rivatives) what actions are "mortally" sinful and what
are only "venially" sinful; at the same time, we attached guilt feelings to those actions most stressed as
sinful by our parents, teachers, and others who influenced us.

But at the same time we were absorbing many other
norms for action from our parents, schools, peer groups,
etc. and gradually working out a more or less conscious
hierarchy of values to be pursued, goals to be achieved,
and acceptable ways of achieving them. These values
and goals, though influenced to some extent by our religious training, were certainly not totally formed by it.

Most of us are, consequently, living at the same time
by a strict code-morality, motivated by fear of losing
God's love and going to hell, and also by the norms we
have absorbed from our society or from particular persons or trends.

Now, it seems that somewhat the same process has
been at work in the development of moral theology in
the Church through the centuries. Every human society
develops and inculcates in its young certain norms of
what must be done or not done in order to protect the
well-being, as it is understood, of the society and its
members. The Ten Commandments condense much of
the accumulated wisdom of mankind as to basic "do's"
and "don'ts" and are presented in scripture as God's
gift of love to His people, showing them how to follow
his "way," in which their own well-being was to be
found. Their obedience was to be their loving response
to his love and care, in the covenant he had established
with them.

Unfortunately, by the time of Christ, the Pharisees
had developed this law, intended to be one of love, into

an intolerable burden of legalism. Jesus' whole point, if one may so express it, was to restore the primacy of love, the attitude of positive concern for one's own and one's neighbor's truly human well-being, as the final norm of human conduct, with "the Law" understood as providing guidelines as to how to achieve this well-being.

But, when early Christian generations felt the need of further explicating the guidelines provided by the Old and New Testaments, they turned to what was apparently the best wisdom of their time, that of the Stoics, who had worked out a theory of behavior very consciously based on what seemed to be conducive to human welfare. The Stoics analyzed the purpose of man's various organs and faculties: the digestive system for nourishing, the genital organs for reproducing, the intellect for seeking truth, the will for seeking goodness, etc. To act rightly, human beings must use each of these organs or faculties to achieve its specific purpose and nothing else. In other words, these must be used in obedience to the "natural laws," the law built into human nature by its very constitution.

But in the Greek perspective, which considered the body as a separate entity from the soul, only a physical, biological purpose could be considered for man's physical organs and processes. To limit the "purpose" of physical acts in this fashion contradicts the scriptural view of man and that of modern psychology and philosophy (and of St. Thomas' basic idea of man as well). It also goes against all ordinary human experience. We do not eat merely to nourish ourselves physically; eating together, for instance, may nourish our whole psychophysical selves, making manifest and creating love and community.

However, even though traditional versions of the "natural law" have seemed to ban organic transplants, voluntary sterilization, etc., as well as contraception, explorations of the "natural law" (in the sense of what does "becoming more fully human" mean) are certainly urgently needed today if we are to make a humanizing, rather than de-humanizing use of present and future scientific advances.

It is, of course, this limited view of the "natural" and, consequently, moral use of human powers that has provided the explicit philosophical basis for the Church's ban on contraception. Its implicit basis is the dislike and distrust of the body and matter as essentially opposed to the soul and the spiritual realm discussed earlier. This belief was never, and never could be, an explicit tenet of Christianity. However, to say that human beings must use their physical and spiritual powers for their God-intended purposes certainly seems in harmony with basic Christian teaching, and has been very much a part of Western Christian thinking for a long time.

We suggest, therefore, that anyone who is still convinced that contraception is intrinsically evil ask himself whether he first learned about "the facts of life" in a context which made babies seem good and desirable, but the sexual organs and intercourse seem beastly, dirty, shameful, unpleasant, or embarrassing. Consequently, did he not first *feel* that contraception must be immoral and then find that the "natural law" as taught to him gave a rational explanation of this feeling? (This was our own experience. We should never have dreamed of practicing contraception, not because the Church said it was wrong, but because we *felt* it was wrong. We first began to think our way out of this feeling when somebody asked us: *Why* do you feel it is wrong?)

From early times, then, Christian preaching and teaching attempted to guide people's behavior in accordance with the "natural law." But, obviously, the interpretation of what is "natural" in the concrete is inevitably greatly influenced by cultural factors. We would think of slavery, or the burning of heretics, as opposed to the natural law today, if we thought in those terms, but for many centuries Christians did not do so.

At the same time, "positive" Church law was developed, that is, laws made by the Church for Christians, like the Sunday Mass observance obligation. Since the Church made these laws, it could change them—as the Friday abstinence law was recently changed—and they are only binding on Christians. But since the "natural law" is God's law, the Church can only interpret it, not change it, and it is binding on all human beings. (This is why Church authorities feel entitled to concern themselves with civil abortion laws, for instance.)

Both the Old Testament and the New bind ethics to religion in such an intimate fashion that the prerequisite to acceptable worship is justice, mercy, and reconciliation with one's neighbor; one cannot love God unless one loves one's neighbor. And, certainly, Scripture teaches that God will punish those who injure others. But in the early Church, specific ecclesiastical punishments or penances were decreed for such serious sins as apostasy, or scandal-giving adultery—penances such as excommunication from the Christian community for a certain period, fasting, etc.

The science of moral theology as we know it today developed from this assigning of specific penances for specific sins. When the practice of private Confession began to spread (at first from the monks in Ireland), confessors wanted authoritative assistance in estimating how gravely a penitent had sinned so that they could give him a proportionate penance. Manuals were therefore compiled with lists of grave and less grave sins and the proper penances for each. As time went on, theologians continued to analyze in greater detail and in response to new questions what actions are to be considered objectively sinful and to what degree and also the subjective conditions required for a person to commit mortal sin, defined as an offense so serious as to kill the true life of the soul, or grace.

In part, at least, because "grace" had come to be thought of in these terms, as a kind of ontological life that one could lose, it seemed vitally important to the teaching Church to inform people about the difference between mortal and venial sin and different kinds of sins. (Look at the Baltimore Catechism, for instance, and see how much of it is, in one way or another, devoted to sin.) As a result, most of us were brought up in a "How far can I go before I commit mortal sin?" mentality, rather than in a positive one: "How can I act most lovingly in the present situation?"

But now, once again, Christians are attempting to reestablish the primacy of love as the ultimate norm of human conduct. This is the basis of the so-called "new morality." But it is not new at all. Jesus himself explicitly proclaimed love of God and neighbor as the two great commandments. The New Testament, as we saw earlier, describes what love really involves. And, among the Greek philosophers who so greatly influenced Christian thinking, Aristotle enunciated the general principle of implementing love: to act so as to achieve the greatest good for the greatest number.

Here, then, is the function of the moral precepts set out by the Church's teaching authorities of the past and present: to guide people in making decisions as to which course of action is most loving, which will achieve the "greatest good of the greatest number." We are not asked to make ethical decisions in a void, but as members of the human race, of a particular cultural community, of the Christian community, and of the Catholic community in particular. The Ten Commandments, the teachings of the Church and of all Christian churches, the human wisdom of the past and present give us the benefit of a vast experience beyond our own to help us decide what, here and now, will actually harm or benefit ourselves and others.[3]

Thus the "new morality" does not do away with the moral law or the authority of Christian teaching. It shows how to use them properly, as elements to be taken into serious consideration in making a moral decision. This view of the role of such laws and precepts in coming to a decision is not new either. In discussing the virtue of prudence, that is, the ability to make right decisions, St. Thomas lists eight elements (1) to learn the facts; (2) to determine the underlying values and issues involved; (3) to reason logically; (4) to take advice; (5) to proceed step by step; (6) to make sure that all the relevant factors have been taken into account; (7) to foresee the consequences of one or another possible course of action; (8) to use one's own inventiveness and resourcefulness in arriving at a final solution and decision. In this listing the role of the moral law and its interpretation through Christian teaching, past and present, would come under (2) and (4). But (8) is essential too: the person's own individual contribution, his own insight, which weighs and fuses all these other elements in coming to a truly personal decision for which the person himself is responsible.

As St. Thomas saw it, this virtue of prudence is the "chamberlain" to wisdom, the ability to perceive where true happiness lies for oneself and others. And wisdom in turn serves love, the queen of all virtues. Thus the "new morality" is simply urging us to follow St. Thomas, to cultivate the virtue of prudence in the service of enlightened love.

In this perspective, current discussions about the degree of authoritativeness of *Humanae Vitae* are relevant only to what degree of serious consideration Catholics should give its teaching, among all the elements to be considered in coming to a decision. Authority, even that of the Pope and a long-standing tradition in the Church, is only one of these elements; although a very important one for the Catholic, it cannot properly usurp the role of all the rest.

On the other hand, nobody attempting to live by the "new morality," as it is being developed within the Catholic tradition, would act against the explicit teaching of the Church, or the Pope—let alone against moral norms generally accepted in the Christian or the human community—without very serious consideration, including an examination of his own motivations in so acting. For the "new morality" urges us to bring the light of human and Christian wisdom to bear on the concrete decisions we have to make.

Thus to "form" one's conscience means not only to acquaint ourselves with the general principles and precepts of Christian teaching and human wisdom in all areas of conduct. It also means to cultivate the habit of bringing all the elements involved in making a wise decision to bear on a given situation, and then to make a decision, and "follow one's conscience." It has consistently been Christian teaching that we are to follow our consciences, having made a serious effort to form them. The peculiar Catholic problem today is that to "form" one's conscience has too often been reduced simply to "asking Father," and "following one's conscience" reduced to following Father's advice.

But thus to form and follow our consciences is much more demanding than simply doing what we are told. It involves examining the whole value-structure by which we are actually living, the norms we are actually observing. It involves learning as much as we can about human nature—our own and others—and about human relationships. It involves finding out as much as one can about the whole context—personal, social economic, political—of our own situation and that of our society. It means training ourselves to act effectively in implementing our good intentions. In other words, it means trying to mature as a loving person, and to implement our love "in deed and truth."

With regard to sexual behavior, for example, the question now becomes: "Am I trying to treat this other person as a person, seeking his or her good as well as my own, in the context of our total situation, present and future?" To attempt seriously to answer this question, people need much more than "sex education" in the narrow sense.

To apply all this to any given couple's decision as to whether or not to practice contraception: They certainly should take into account the teaching of the Church and the Pope's recent reiteration of it in their historical context. They should consider very deeply the positive thrust of Christian teaching in favor of life, qualitatively as well as quantitatively. (To be antilife in either sense is, surely, the enduring meaning of the "contraceptive mentality" feared by the Church.) They should also consider their own physical and mental health, their relationship and its growth, the bringing up of their children (present and/or future) as loving, maturing persons, their obligations present and future, their role in society. They also need to take into account the effectiveness, acceptability and ultimate healthfulness of available methods of contraception (and the fact that none is as yet 100 per cent effective or satisfactory). They should bring all these considerations to bear in making their personal decision as to whether or not practicing contraception here and now will best help them and their children to mature as loving, creative persons in today's society. In sum, they need seriously to think out: Which will be the more loving course of action in these concrete circumstances?

One cannot sincerely begin to try to form one's conscience along the lines of a love-centered mentality with regard to sexual behavior alone. Of its nature, this effort must become a total, life-extensive, and lifelong struggle to become a more loving person and to act more lovingly. It involves the deepening realization of one's selfishness, one's unlovingness, in attitude and in action. It involves many "conversions," in the sense of calls to change of heart, as one realizes how self-centered and unloving one has been in some area of life. The need for repentance, reparation, and the sacrament of Penance is evident in this new outlook.

But the focus is very different. One cannot continue to think in the mortal sin-venial sin terms in which we were brought up. Certainly it must be possible to turn away from divine and human love so completely as to reject God completely. But how often and to what extent are we so completely ourselves that such a total rejection is possible? In any case, is the concept of "grace" as an entity added on to human life without which one cannot "enter heaven" the only authentically Christian expression of the reality of the relationship God wishes to enter into with us? Do we have to believe that this "life of grace" was given to our first parents, lost at the Fall, restored to us by Christ's atoning death, is given to individuals at Baptism and restored (if it is lost by mortal sin) through perfect contrition and the sacrament of Penance? Can we really believe that the God who so loved the world as to give us his Son actually deals with us in these terms? Still more, can we really believe that, if God loves men so much, he does not care about the quality of human life on earth, about what we do with our lives and our talents, that he is only concerned about getting souls safely to heaven?

The answer given by the *whole* tradition of the Church and by modern theological developments is, certainly, that this is only one expression of the realities of the faith, and a very minimal and legalistic one.[4] The historical factors involved in the transformation of the gospel into this kind of security-oriented "pie in the sky" religion, which keeps people contented with the *status quo*, are too complicated to go into here. But the point is that Catholics who are still sincerely living in this doctrinal framework cannot accept the "new morality" for themselves or others or take the risk involved in making personal moral decisions about contraception or anything else. To do so simply does not make sense. If the purpose of human life is assumed to be that individual "souls" in as great numbers as possible should avoid hell, then the authorities of the Church must try to form, protect, and even coerce people on earth for their own everlasting well-being in heaven. And, equally, Catholics do not need to ask questions, to make decisions, to try to change social conditions (unless these are detrimental to the functioning of the Church). It is far safer not to do anything more than "pay, pray, and obey."

The Second Vatican Council took great steps toward renouncing this view of Christian faith and life, particularly in its *Constitution on the Church in the Modern World.* And now, increasingly, theological developments are restoring the scriptural perspectives of Christian faith. We are to work and struggle and suffer to help one another toward fullness of life, toward community in love with one another and with God. This is the human vocation, to which all men are called. The mission of the Church and its members is to proclaim, primarily through loving service and a loving life-style, that in Christ God is with and for mankind in this struggle and will bring about its ultimate success, beyond human dreams, in the Kingdom fully come.

But this hope is an incentive to action, not passivity. Precisely because we have this hope, we cannot give up struggling for a better life for all human persons. It is the despairing who cease to act, not the hopeful— and this is why we try to share our Christian hope. Christianity, then, is not meant to offer people security in exchange for rule-keeping. It is an invitation to lay down our lives in loving service, to help one another toward the fullness of life that Christ came to make possible for mankind and of which he is the witness and guarantee.

In such a vision of the purpose of human life and history and the mission of Christians in relation to it love-centered morality makes sense. In fact, it is the only properly human kind of morality, oriented towards the free and responsible human maturity of those who follow it. And it is in the context of such a morality that "following one's conscience" makes sense.

The issue of the morality of contraception, therefore, as raised in today's situation, necessarily raises these broader and deeper issues as well. We believe that the interrelationship of these issues needs to be brought out and discussed as often as possible and as clearly as possible for the good of Catholics who are disturbed about contraception and for those who are not, and for the good of the whole Church.

NOTES

1. We have tried to set out the results of our own study and effort through some twenty-five years of married life in our book, *Love and Sexuality. A Christian Approach* (Holt, Rinehart and Winston, 1967).

2. In the Bible, "spirit" does not mean something "without a body." It means the aliveness of anything, what makes it live (derived from the Latin or Greek or Hebrew root-words for "breath"). Thus God, the supremely alive One, is supremely "Spirit"; the Lord Jesus became "Spirit" at his resurrection and now pours out the Spirit to enable men to love more fully and live more fully (cf. John 10:10; 1 John 14).

3. For a brief and helpful treatment, see *How Do I Know I'm Doing Right?*, by Gerard S. Sloyan (booklet, Geo. A. Pflaum Co., 1967); also *Toward Moral Maturity*, ed. by Mary Perkins Ryan (booklet, The Paulist Press, 1968, containing articles from *The Living Light*, by Daniel Maguire, David O'Neill, etc.)

4. See *What Do We Really Believe?*, by Richard P. McBrien (booklet, Geo. A. Pflaum Co., 1969).

10

A Catholic Pediatrician on Family Planning

◆◆◆

Thomas F. Draper, M.D.

Until 1800 the practice of medicine was largely a mixture of superstition, sorcery, and primitive surgery. However, in the nineteenth century man made his first great strides in the control of disease, first providing sanitary services in the management of his environment, then in the discovery of bacteria as a cause of infection. Since that time the profession of medicine has matured in its understanding of the scope and meaning of disease, and society at large has come to expect remedies for the ills that it suffers. In the United States today it is expected that if a child can be paralyzed by poliomyelitis, the disease should be prevented, if a premature infant can suffer blindness, the cause should be found, and if a child cannot learn in school, the causative factors should be identified and dealt with. In short, medicine has come to measure its effectiveness by the level of capability at which its patients can function in society.

As control of infectious disease has improved by more efficient sanitation, immunizing agents and antibiotics, the physician has broadened his concern from mere survival of his patients to an acceptance of responsibility for the kind and quality of human life in his care. Infirmity, physical or emotional, that impairs the optimal function of a child is recognized by the pediatrician as proper subject for his effort and study. The fundamental role of the environment in the manifestation of disease has caused the pediatrician to be concerned at once with the community and the child in the community, the school and the child in the school, the family and the child in the family.

In appraising the ills of society, social scientists are fond of pointing to "gaps," rich-poor, black-white, old-young, as symptoms of social sickness. Fragmentation is viewed as a measure of social decay. The physician to the family, be he G.P., pediatrician, or internist, sees the family as the unit cell of society; he understands that fragmentation within the family may manifest itself in the children by school failure, deviant behavior, or delinquency.

It is common for physicians to participate with families in seeking solutions to marriage problems. In reviewing the histories of twelve fragmenting Catholic families with whom I was associated, I found that there were sixty-six children involved, that no family had less than four children, and that as of this writing, two of the marriages terminated in divorce (eleven children). The causes of the conflicts confronted by families in which the presence of multiple children was associated not with an increase in family love, but with hostility, resentment and anger, has been the source of continuing speculation. Do children not have a right to parental love, a right to be wanted? Can parents who do not love each other provide an environment favorable to child rearing? In the absence of a climate of love ought there not be an obligation for parents to cease having additional children? If interparent distrust, disharmony and disrespect compromise the growth and functioning of the offspring, ought not the family physician to seek the causes of the psychological and emotional handicap to the child and pursue its therapy and prevention?

It is not possible to typify the "problem" family. However, certain themes emerge as characteristic of this small group. Most commonly the marriage was between two Catholics, the girl in her early twenties, the boy a few years older. The spouses anticipated families of four or more children and were anxious for the early occurence of the first pregnancy. After the arrival of the first baby, the parents tried to delay the second and subsequent pregnancies by the rhythm method (periodic continence). Among all of these families, rhythm was unsuccessful and considered by them as a major contributor to their friction. The words of one such mother recently interviewed are revealing:

I had five children in six years. We had wanted the first baby right away and I do love all of my children. But when the last one was born, our fifth, I had "that terrible feeling" that I couldn't take care of any of the children. I couldn't take care of the house; I couldn't cook the meals; I couldn't even change the baby. I didn't want to look at any of the children. I couldn't leave the room; I just stayed there and cried. I think I should have been in the hospital. For almost a year my husband, neighbors, and friends took care of everything. Life seemed hopeless, babies would keep coming and I would be unable to take care of them. I think I wanted to die. Then a doctor prescribed some birth control pills, but two priests told me I wasn't allowed to take them. Someone told me of a priest who would give permission. I went to him and he told me that it was like taking aspirin. I didn't believe him, but I took the pills.

I asked this woman what effect taking these pills actually had on her life. Her own words are apt:

"The first six years of my married life were torment. I wasn't a wife. I was afraid to give myself to my husband. I was afraid of intercourse because it meant pregnancy. I resented my husband coming home at night. I was afraid to smile at him, to show affection, even to hold his hand lest it lead to something more. Now I can smile again. I think all I ever want to do is make my husband happy. When he's happy, I'm happy and the children are happy.

A mother of six observed of her family life:

I think that marriage ought to be based on love, you ought to love the one you marry. I think that love is communication, understanding, compassion. I think my principal responsibility is to raise my children in a proper way—to respect others—to understand the works of God—to meet their responsibilities to their fellow man. I think that families should eat together because that helps them to love each other. I think that family problems have to be settled privately. But I honestly feel now I've reached my capacity. Our oldest is eight and the youngest only two. I don't seem able to communicate with all of the children as individuals. There doesn't seem to be enough time. I can't love them the way I want to. I can't find the privacy to deal with their personal problems. I seem to lack patience. I'm always

fatigued. I can't discipline them. We practiced rhythm for
the last four children. It was a nightmare. It bred distrust
and hate of the very one you love. You live by the calendar, under the constant threat that the whole world will
collapse if there's another pregnancy. I know the pills
aren't the answer, but at least they've given me a chance
to breathe.

What is the answer? Or indeed is there an answer at
all. The problem that seems to be recurrent is this:
That love is fundamental to the successful maturation
of the family. That love is dynamic and must grow to
survive. That somehow it is measured by communication and understanding and compassion. That its growth
within the family is dependent upon its growth between
the parents and propagated among the children and that
by this love mutual confidence and respect is bred
among the members of the family. That in the environment of love, mutual respect, and confidence, the education of all the members of the family occurs. Any
factor that diminishes or destroys this love compromises
the intellectual, emotional, and social development of
the family and moves them in the direction of fragmentation.

In medicine, it is recognized that the same disease
may manifest itself in different ways in different people.
So too in the fragmenting family, the manifest symptom
may be the delinquent child rather than the problem
marriage. Whether the initiative arise from law en-
forcement agencies, school authorities, or the parents,
children manifesting deviant or delinquent behavior are
frequently referred to the family physician for appraisal.

The Committee on Juvenile Delinquency of the

American Pediatric Society has characterized the families of delinquent children as (1) lacking warm parent-child relationship; (2) lacking maternal supervision; (3) lacking completely or partially presence of the father. In discussing problems of delinquency the Gluecks suggested five criteria of family life that they utilize to forecast juvenile delinquency with considerable accuracy. These criteria are: discipline of boy by father; supervision by mother; affection by father; affection by mother; cohesiveness of family. In so far as delinquent behavior is symptomatic of family malaise, the causes of delinquency are important to the physician concerned with family well-being. Parents find no difficulty in comprehending the Glueck criteria. But the father who requires a second job to support a growing number of children often lacks time and energy to discipline his son, or show affection for his children. An unlimited number of children may well exceed the capacity of a mother to supervise the individual care of each of the children.

The change from rural living in this country to urban industrial life has profoundly affected the family. The parents of earlier generations raised their children with or near their ancestors. At an early age on the farm these children contributed to its productivity. Today's family has become a "single cell" unit, often remote from collaterals and ancestors. The care and raising of these children has become a task for the man and wife alone with little help from other kin. And these children remain in a dependent status in the home pursuing formal education often for twenty years or more. The 1968 mother cannot ask her mother to care for an infant while she attempts to unravel the problems of a

high school or college age offspring. The mother of
today must be prepared to deal at once with infant,
school child, or teenager. Today's father cannot share
his occupation in support of his family with a son as
did his farming ancestor. He must support that son
for a far longer and costlier time. In meeting these complex responsibilities the parents find there comes a time
when increasing the family compromises their capacity
to meet their responsibilities to the existing children.
When that moment is reached, additional babies intro-
duce strain and tension and serve to diminish the cohesion of the family unit.

A thirty-five-year-old mother of four small children
was convinced that her husband no longer loved her.
They had not had conjugal relations for months; he was
spending far more time at work than before and when
not working seemed to find endless reasons for being
out of the home. On rare occasions when they would
be out socially he would find excuses to leave her and
visit with others. In additon he had established a favor-
ite among the children and lavished most of his attention on this one child to the jealousy of the others.
He was critical of every effort expended by the mother
in the care of home and children. The mother felt she
was a failure, rejected, and that their marriage was
threatened by decay. After discussion with the father it
was revealed that he was so fearful of being unable to
care for additional children that he became resentful of
his wife's affection and repulsed her every effort to
please him. Intercourse meant another baby: His wife
became a threat to his security. Hate was replacing
love, only this time it was the man who feared showing
any affection to his wife. As a consequence, the fatherly

love for the other children was distorted, his presence in the home diminished, and the cohesion of the family was threatened.

The American Catholic family of today shares the strain of all family life in our society but in addition bears a burden that is unique. In a worldly environment of hostility, anger, crime, and war, the family recognizes the special obligation to nurture love. In meeting this responsibility some families have found that this love may be threatened or destroyed by further increase in family size. In ministering to the ills of families it has been my experience that when responsibilities become excessive, the warm parent-child relationship is threatened, the love between the spouses is devoured by fear and the cohesion of the family may succumb to separation or divorce. As one particularily concerned with the community, I recognize family love as the bedrock upon which society must build. Therefore I conclude that in those instances where family planning may contribute to the preservation of family life, this service must be provided.

11

The Encyclical

A nun in Washington D.C. gave *N.C.R.* a bit of help last week by letting one of our stringers use the photocopying machine in her office. Offered payment, she declined. "I'll just pray that you won't be too hard on the Pope," she said.

This is the same Pope who wrote *The Progress of Peoples*, who came to the U.N. in New York and pleaded for an end of war, who visited Palestine and India, welcomed an Anglican primate and an Orthodox patriarch to the Vatican, tried to end the war in Vietnam, is giving strong help to the people of Biafra. Nobody wants to be hard on him. Everybody knows the birth control decision was terribly difficult for him, and that he was as conscientious about it as he could be.

From other sources, other advice. *Don't overreact.*

* An editorial from *National Catholic Reporter,* Aug. 7, 1968.

We'll try not to. *Read the encyclical with sympathy; find the values the Pope is defending.* The values are there; one must honor them to understand what the Pope is saying.

The encyclical affirms the sacredness of human life, an ultimate among good things. It rightly extends this sacredness to the act of love which begets life. It rightly assumes that when people use contraceptives in their lovemaking, a moral question is posed. Even the unobtrusive pill works a basic change in a fundamental human encounter: By the choice and initiative of the partners, their coupling no longer has anything to do with having children. Is this change good, bad or neutral? That is a good question. No one can evaluate the Pope's letter who does not acknowledge its validity, the need for an answer.

Finally, there is something to be said on behalf of the encyclical's approach to the job of giving an answer. Most of us live most of our lives by a morality of consequences, so that we readily understand the standard defense of contraception which says the pill (for example) is available, solves serious problems, hurts nobody and therefore is moral. But contraception could be wrong and yet have some good effects—as did the bombing of Hiroshima. Not all the effects of human actions can be observed or measured—how will a sociologist weigh an obvious easing of anxiety in some couples against a subtle growth of selfishness and pleasure-seeking in others? Again: the psychological benefits of contraception are vividly experienced, but if there is a purpose built into marital relations which is mutilated by contraception, this effect need not reach the level of consciousness to be real. And such a mutilation of sex and marriage, if that is what it is, eventually will affect the whole tone of civilization, whether or not the result can be readily traced to the cause.

The way the Pope argues the question follows an ancient and intellectually respectable tradition. It rises above statistics and relies upon analysis; it tries to reach the *meaning* of the act of love. Such an approach is necessarily abstract, therefore uncongenial to the pragmatic modern mind; a factor that must be kept in mind in weighing its persuasiveness. For many Catholics, another and more powerfully negative factor is the unwelcome conclusion the argument reaches; that too is a factor that should be discounted. For, as practically every theologian who has expressed a view on the encyclical has stressed, it is part of the meaning of being a Catholic that one gives respectful and close attention to the teaching of the Pope. That includes trying to understand the mode and form of the argument so as to grasp whatever force it may have, and it includes a willingness to subordinate self-interest and to purge oneself of bias.

And yet, as many of these same theologians have also said in one phrasing or another, the Catholic understanding of obedience to the Pope does not require anyone to do violence to his own mind. Self-administered brain-washing is not a Catholic exercise. The Catholic honestly concerned to form his conscience rightly in this matter should give due weight to the authority of the Pope, should give fair consideration to the power of his presentation; but if for serious reasons he then finds himself unable to assent to this teaching he is not bound to accept it either intellectually or in practice. And, since the teaching is not presented as infallible, his withholding of assent does not make him less a Catholic, either in his own estimation or in the "external forum."

The example of the theologians suggests also that silent nonconcurrence is not the only option; that, in fact, there can be an obligation to be vocal. That has always been the case, but—especially in the interval between the First and Second Vatican Councils—we haven't heard much about episodes in Catholic history or elements of Catholic teaching having to do with the duty of responsible dissent.

In the present instance, despite what was said earlier, we believe such dissent is called for. Several commentators have said that the encyclical creates a crisis of credibility for the papacy. It also creates a crisis of collegiality for the church.

The source of both crises is the content of the encyclical, together with the mode of its preparation and the context within which it is published. This is not merely a matter of a predictably unpopular ruling. The unprecedented critical reaction the encyclical has engendered will of course be blamed on hedonism among the laity and intellectual pride among the theologians; but it should not be. No doubt some of the protestors are oversexed and some are snobs, but that does not account for the number, force or quality of the criticisms.

The reason for the reaction is rather that the birth control issue poses a serious question and the encyclical does not give a serious answer. Even if it is read sympathetically, with all the caveats outlined above kept carefully in mind, it falls very far short of justifying the teaching it attempts to convey.

Catholic teaching on contraception affects the lives of millions of married Catholics everywhere. It influences the population policies of governments and of the United Nations, as well as the personal decision of hundreds of thousands of couples in countries which desperately need to curb their population growth to prevent economic stagnation, malnutrition and starvation. Finally, this encyclical purports to express the mind of Catholicism on sex in marriage; by failing to present a respectable rationale for the stand it takes, it imposes an impossible burden on Catholic teachers and confessors and creates a formidable new obstacle to theological exchange with other churches.

These of course are mere declarations; some analysis in support is called for.

Ultimately, the entire weight of the encyclical rests on a single assertion, to the effect that there exists an *"inseparable connection, willed by God and unable to be broken by man on his own initiative, between the two meanings of the conjugal act: the unitive meaning and the procreative meaning"* (par. 12). This is not a ridiculous statement; it is a serious attempt to state the meaning of sexuality in marriage, and there are competent philosophers who consider it a profound insight. But, as Father Richard McCormick points out, the principle is already familiar to theologians, many of whom find it "extremely difficult to sustain." Obviously, in the ordinary course of things there is a connection between the unitive and procreative meanings of intercourse, between making love and making babies. But is the connection *inseparable*? How do we *know* that it is inseparable? On what basis is it asserted that separating the two functions of the marital act, by means of contraception, is *evil*?

These are not only permissible but required questions, questions of a kind that a rational human being ought to ask about any statement proposed to him as a guide of moral conduct. The encyclical does not answer them. It offers several variant formulations of the same basic proposition; but no proof is given, no solid indication is made of the line of reasoning which leads to this conclusion, no scriptural texts are cited in its support. There are hints, but no more (pars. 11, 12, 13) of arguments drawn from human biological structures and from the procreative character of marriage, or from a convergence of the two. But the argument from bodily arrangements was discarded long ago as mechanistic; the structure of the body does not of itself reveal the proper use of the body. The "procreation is primary" view of marriage was abandoned at Vatican II.

As in every other defense of the traditional teaching, the attempt to justify the rhythm method while condemning contraception makes for problems. The encyclical says that marital acts during the infertile period are lawful, though no child can be conceived, because the wife's cycle occurs independently of the partners' wills—these acts, then, "remain ordained toward expressing and consolidating" the union of the partners. Every marriage act "must remain open to the transmission of life"; acts taking place during the infertile period are said to be thus "open" and they do not violate the "inseparable connection" as would acts of contraceptive intercourse, which require purposeful initiative. Inserting a diaphragm to insure infertility is against God's will. Observing a calendar or a thermometer to take advantage of natural fertility is acceptable.

It is not legitimate to reject this argument solely on the ground that one does not understand it. But it seems strange that so important a moral principle would be so difficult to grasp, and that it would receive so little corroboration from the experience of married persons.

On the more fundamental point, that contraception is evil because it breaks an unbreakable link, the only real corroboration the encyclical provides is an appeal to authority: "This is what the church has always taught." Paragraph 6 indicates that members of the majority group in the papal birth control commission were mistaken if they thought their mission was to re-examine and reinterpret the church's traditional stand; their report recommending a change was found unsatisfactory precisely because it suggested new criteria for solutions to the birth control question, criteria differing from "the moral teaching on marriage proposed with constant firmness by the teaching authority of the church."

The reason all this is critically important is that the encyclical makes no pretense of finding authority in God's revelation for stating that contraception is against God's will. The teaching is founded on natural law, the encyclical says. To discover the natural law requires the use of reason, to explain and defend it requires the presentation of arguments drawn from reason. But to say that contraception is sinful because it separates what is inseparable is not powerfully persuasive; it says little more than: Contraception is wrong because what it does is bad. Pope Paul is surely mistaken when he expresses a belief that "the men of our day are peculiarly capable of seizing the deeply reasonable and human character" of the encyclical's guiding principle. If that were the case the Roman Catholic church would not be virtually alone among major religious bodies in rejecting contraception as evil. In fact the men of our day find the teaching incomprehensible—and rather sad. We are gifted with a natural law doctrine that has a touch of the esoteric about it, an insight that can be achieved for the most part only by Catholics, and most easily by Catholic celibates of a certain age. As Father Häring notes, some of them find the teaching so clear and vital that they can enforce it against mothers on their return from mental hospitals to which they have been driven by too many pregnancies too closely grouped.

The focus of these comments, it should be noted, is not on the issue itself—is contraception good or bad? —but on the key reasons offered by the encyclical for saying it is bad. The aim here is not to prove that artificial birth control is good, but only to weigh whether the encyclical makes a reasonable case for calling it evil, for telling Catholics that it is sinful. We conclude that it does not make such a case. Many readers will believe the conclusion was foreordained; we hope they will address themselves to the arguments rather than to personalities.

The crisis of credibility is occasioned by the sheer inadequacy of the encyclical, coupled with the gravity of the issue, the amount of time, effort and expertise given to preparation, and the encyclical's internal self-bolstering statements requiring the internal and external assent of theologians and pastors.

It is already evident that a very considerable number of the church's professional class will not be able to give him this assent. For the Pope, who has already suffered greatly under the cross of this decision, such a response will impose sheer agony. For the church, the crisis of credibility can well be the occasion of a great purification.

The nature of the purification is suggested by the contrast between the statements issued by Msgr. Austin Vaughan, president of the American Catholic Theological society, and Dr. Germain Grisez of Georgetown, on the one hand, and, on the other, those drawn up by such men as Fathers Bernard Häring and Richard McCormick and the Washington group led by Father Charles Curran.

Dr. Grisez said that to be a Catholic is to be a papist, and a papist cannot say "Rome has spoken but the cause goes on." Msgr. Vaughan wrote: "Every man must follow his conscience, but a Catholic accepts the guidance of the church as an obligatory way of forming his conscience."

In contrast, Father McCormick: ". . . (L)oyalty to the magisterium cannot be defined in terms merely of theological acquiescence. Indeed the theologian sees this as potentially the ultimate form of disloyalty. Reverence and respect for the magisterium allow for and demand criticism, even dissent, when this is done charitably and responsibly."

The Curran group: "It is common teaching in the church that Catholics may dissent from authoritative, non-infallible teachings of the magisterium when sufficient reasons for so doing exist."

In our judgment the Vaughan-Grisez approach reflects a sort of Byzantine ideal of total submission which has always been around in the church but became exaggerated after Vatican I. But the McCormick-Curran emphasis is not a recent, post-Vatican II arrival—it too has always been around; it could be supported out of Thomas Aquinas. Statements by the magisterium have always inflated the "ordinary teaching authority," making its interim pronouncements in effect all but indistinguishable from the central dogmas of the faith. And there have usually been some theologians or even bishops to reassert the rights of conscience, scholarship and common sense.

In the American Church the Byzantine approach once held most of the high ground; it has been losing sway of late but still grips a great portion of the laity and a considerable number of priests. The *Humanae Vitae* incident will favor recovery of greater freedom, especially among lay people. The cost of the process will be determined by the bishops. If they are rigorous in enforcing compliance with the encyclical, firing or silencing pastors and professors, the cost will be high. They will do it if they continue to identify the church with the Pope, if they feel they have to rally around even when he acts anti-collegially and arbitrarily.

The purification will be less painful if the bishops understand that loyalty to the church and to Christ may occasionally call on them to criticize the Pope and even to resist him; if they understand that theologians like McCormick got their ideas about personal conscience not out of the secularist, decadent modern *Zeitgeist* but from the Gospel; if they understand that the church will never be truly collegial unless they throw their own weight around a bit and let their priests do the same.

If that happens, the crisis of collegiality will be solved along with the crisis of credibility. On the other hand, we could be seeing a much smaller church pretty soon, with a lot of the best people in it gone to other pastures or underground.

Part III

12

Majority Papal
Commission Report

———————◆◆◆———————

*This document represents the culmination of the work
of the papal birth control commission. Its authors
are the Rev. Joseph Fuchs, German Jesuit teaching at
the Gregorian university in Rome; the Rev. Raymond
Sigmond, Hungarian Dominican, president of the Institute of Social Science of the Pontifical University of
St. Thomas Aquinas; the Rev. Paul Anciaux, professor
at the major seminary of Malines-Brussels, Belgium;
the Rev. A. Auer, specialist in sexual questions, Wurz-
burg Germany; the Rev. Michel Labourdette, O.P.,
theologian from Toulouse, France, and the Rev. Pierre
do Locht of the National Family Pastorial Center,
Brussels. Thirteen other theologians and several experts
from other fields also signed the document. The report's final wording was worked out in the commission's*

* From *National Catholic Reporter*, April 19, 1967.

*last plenary meeting, held June 4–9, 1966. Its Latin
title is:* "Schema Documenti de Responsabili Paterni-
tate": *"Schema for a Document on Responsible Parenthood."*

INTRODUCTION

*The Pastoral Constitution on the Church in the Mod-
ern World (Gaudium et Spes)* has not explained the
question of responsible parenthood under all its aspects.
To those problems as yet unresolved, a response is to
be given in what follows. This response, however, can
only be understood if it is grasped in an integrated
way within the universal concept of salvation history.

In creating the world God gave man the power and
the duty to form the world in spirit and freedom and,
through his creative capacity, to actuate his own personal nature. In his Word, God himself, as the first
efficient cause of the whole evolution of the world and
of man, is present and active in history. The story of
God and of man, therefore, should be seen as a shared
work. And it should be seen that man's tremendous
progress in control of matter by technical means, and
the universal and total "intercommunication" that has
been achieved, correspond perfectly to the divine de-
crees (cf. *Constitution on the Church in the Modern
World,* I, c.3).

In the fullness of time the Word of the eternal
Father entered into history and took his place within
it, so that by his work humanity and the world might
become sharers in salvation. After his ascension to the
Father, the Lord continues to accomplish his work
through the church. As God became man, so his church

is really incarnate in the world. But because the world, to which the church ought to represent the mystery of Christ, always undergoes changes, the church itself necessarily and continually is in pilgrimage. Its essence and fundamental structures remain immutable always; and yet no one can say of the church that at any time it is sufficiently understood or bounded by definition (cf. Paul VI in *Ecclesiam Suam* and in his opening speech to the second session of Vatican Council II).

The church was constituted in the course of time by Christ, its principle of origin is the Word of creation and salvation. For this reason the church draws understanding of its own mystery not only from the past, but, standing in the present time and looking to the future, assumes within itself, the whole progress of the human race. The church is always being made more sure of this. What John XXIII wished to express by the word "*aggiornamento*," Paul VI took up, using the phrase, "dialogue with the world" and in his encyclical *Ecclesiam Suam* has the following: "The world cannot be saved from the outside. As the Word of God became man, so must a man to a certain degree identify with the forms of life of those to whom he wishes to bring the message of Christ. Without invoking privileges which would but widen the separation, without employing unintelligible terminology, he must share the common way of life—provided that it is human and honorable—especially of the most humble, if he wishes to be listened to and understood" (par.87).

In response to the many problems posed by the changes occurring today in almost every field, the church in Vatican Council II has entered into the way of dialogue. "The church guards the heritage of God's

Word and draws from it religious and moral principles, without always having at hand the solution to particular problems. She desires thereby to add the light of revealed truth to mankind's store of experience, so that the path which humanity has taken in recent times will not be a dark one" (*Constitution on the Church in the Modern World*, I. c.3, par.33).

In fulfillment of its mission the church must propose obligatory norms of human and Christian life from the deposit of faith in an open dialogue with the world. But since moral obligations can never be detailed in all their concrete particularities, the personal responsibility of each individual must always be called into play. This is even clearer today because of the complexity of modern life: the concrete moral norms to be followed must not be pushed to an extreme.

In the present study, dealing with problems relating to responsible parenthood, the Holy Father through his ready willingness to enter into dialogue has given it an importance unprecedented in history. After several years of study, a commission of experts called together by him, made up for the most part of laymen from various fields of competency, has prepared material for him, which was lastly examined by a special group of bishops.

PART I: FUNDAMENTAL PRINCIPLES

Chapter I: The Fundamental Values of Marriage

"The well-being of the individual person and of human and Christian society is intimately linked with the healthy condition of that community produced by marriage and family. Hence Christians and all men who hold this community in high esteem sincerely rejoice in the various ways by which men today find help in fostering this community of love and perfecting its life, and by which spouses and parents are assisted in their lofty calling. Those who rejoice in such aid look for additional benefits from them and labor to bring them about." (*Constitution on the Church in the Modern World*, II, c.1, par.47).

Over the course of centuries, the Church, with the authority conferred it by Christ our Lord, has constantly protected the dignity and essential values of this institution whose author is God himself who has made man to his image and raised him to share in his love. It has always taught this to its faithful and to all men. In our day it again intends to propose to those many families who are seeking a right way how they are able in the conditions of our times to live and develop fully the higher gifts of this community.

A couple (*unio conjugum*) ought to be considered above all a community of persons which has in itself the beginning of new human life. Therefore those things which strengthen and make more profound the union of persons within this community must never be separated from the procreative finality which specifies the conjugal community. Pius XI, in *Casti Connubii* already, referring to the tradition expressed in the Roman Catechism, said: "This mutual inward molding of a husband and wife, this determined effort to perfect each other, can in a very real sense be said to be the chief reason and purpose of matrimony, provided matrimony be looked at not in the restricted sense as instituted for the proper conception and education of the child, but more widely as the blending of life as a whole and the mutual interchange and sharing thereof" (*AAS*, XXII, 1930, p. 547).

But conjugal love, without which marriage would not be a true union of persons, is not exhausted in the simple mutual giving in which one party seeks only the other. Married people know well that they are only able to perfect each other and establish a true community if their love does not end in a merely egotistic union but according to the condition of each is made truly fruitful in the creation of new life. Nor on the other hand can the procreation and education of a child be considered a truly human fruitfulness unless it is the result of a love existing in a family community. Conjugal love and fecundity are in no way opposed, but complement one another in such a way that they constitute an almost indivisible unity.

Unfolding the natural and divine law, the church urges all men to be true dispensers of the divine gifts, to act in conformity with their own personal nature and to shape their married life according to the dictates of the natural and divine law. God created man male and female so that, joined together in the bonds of love, they might perfect one another through a mutual, corporal and spiritual giving and that they might carefully prepare their children, the fruit of this love, for a truly human life. Let them regard one another always as persons and not as mere objects. Therefore everything should be done in marriage so that the goods conferred on this institution can be attained as perfectly as possible and so that fidelity and moral rightness can be served.

*Chapter II: Responsible Parenthood and the
Regulation of Conception*

To cultivate and realize all the essential values of marriage, married people should become ever more deeply aware of the profundity of their vocation and the breadth of their responsibilities. In this spirit and with this awareness let married people seek how they might better be "cooperators with the love of God and Creator and be, so to speak, the interpreters of that love" for the task of procreation and education (*Constitution on the Church in the Modern World,* II, c.1, par.50).

(1) *Responsible parenthood* (that is, generous and prudent parenthood) is a fundamental requirement of a married couple's true mission. Illumined by faith, the spouses understand the scope of their whole task; helped by divine grace, they try to fulfill it as a true service, carried out in the name of God and Christ, oriented to the temporal and eternal good of men. To save, protect and promote the good of the offspring, and thus of the family community and of human society, the married couple will take care to consider all values and seek to realize them harmoniously in the best way they can, with proper reverence toward each other as persons and according to the concrete circumstances of their life. They will make a judgment in conscience before God about the number of children to have and educate according to the objective criteria indicated by Vatican Council II (*Constitution on the Church in the Modern World,* II, c.1, par.50 and c.5, par.80).

This responsible, generous and prudent parenthood always carries with it new demands. In today's situation both because of new difficulties and because of new possibilities for the education of children, couples are hardly able to meet such demands unless with generosity and sincere deliberation.

With a view to the education of children let couples more and more build the community of their whole life on a true and magnanimous love, under the guidance of the spirit of Christ (I Cor.: 12, 31–13,13). For this stable community between man and woman, shaped by conjugal love, is the true foundation of human fruitfulness. This community between married people through which an individual finds himself by opening himself to another, constitutes the optimum situation in which children can be educated in a integrated way. Through developing their communion and intimacy in all its aspects, a married couple is able to provide that environment of love, mutual understanding and humble acceptance which is the necessary condition of authentic human education and maturation.

Responsible parenthood—through which married persons intend to observe and cultivate the essential values of matrimony with a view to the good of persons (the good of the child to be educated, of the couples themselves and of the whole of human society)—is one of the conditions and expressions of a true conjugal chastity. For genuine love, rooted in faith, hope and charity, ought to inform the whole life and every action of a couple. By the strength of this chastity the couple tend to the actuation of that true love precisely inasmuch as it is conjugal and fruitful. They accept generously and prudently their task with all its values, combining them in the best way possible according to the particular circumstances and of their life and in spite of difficulties.

Married people know well that very often they are invited to keep abstinence, and sometimes not just for a brief time, because of the habitual conditions of their life, for example, the good of one of the spouses (physical or psychic well-being), or because of what are called professional necessities. This abstinence a chaste couple know and accept as a condition of progress into a deeper mutual love, fully conscious that the grace of Christ will sustain and strengthen them for this.

Seeing their vocation in all its depth and breadth and accepting it, the couple follows Christ and tries to imitate Him in a true evangelical spirit (MT. 5: 1–12). Comforted by the spirit of Christ according to the inner man and rooted in faith and charity (Eph. 3: 16–17), they try to build up a total life community, "bearing with one another charitably, in complete selflessness, gentleness and patience" (Eph. 4: 2–3. cf. Col: 3, 12–17). They will have the peace of Christ in their hearts and give thanks to God the Father as his holy and elected sons.

A couple then is able to ask and expect that they will be helped by all in such a way that they are progressively able to approach more and more responsible parenthood. They need the help of all in order that they can fulfill their responsibilities with full liberty and in the most favorable material, psychological, cultural and spiritual conditions. By the development of the family, then, the whole society is built up with regard to the good of all men in the whole world.

(2) The *regulation of conception* appears necessary

for many couples who wish to achieve a responsible, open and reasonable parenthood in today's circumstances. If they are to observe and cultivate all the essential values of marriage, married people need decent and human means for the regulation of conception. They should be able to expect the collaboration of all, especially from men of learning and science, in order that they can have at their disposal means agreeable and worthy of man in the fulfilling of his responsible parenthood.

It is proper to man, created to the image of God, to use what is given in physical nature in a way that he may develop it to its full significance with a view to the good of the whole person. This is the cultural mission which the Creator has commissioned to men, whom he has made his cooperators. According to the exigencies of human nature and with the progress of the sciences, men should discover means more and more apt and adequate so that the "ministry which must be fulfilled in a manner which is worthy of man" (*Constitution on the Church in the Modern World*, II, c.1, par.51) can be fulfilled by married people.

This intervention of man into physiological processes, an intervention ordained to the essential values of marriage and first of all to the good of children is to be judged according to the fundamental principles and objective criteria of morality, which will be treated below (in Chap. 4).

"Marriage and conjugal love are by their nature ordained toward the begetting and educating of children" (*Constitution on the Church in the Modern World*, II, c.1, par.50). A right ordering toward the good of the child within the conjugal and familial community pertains to the essence of human sexuality. Therefore the morality of sexual acts between married people takes its meaning first of all and specifically from the ordering of their actions in a fruitful married life, that is one which is practiced with responsible, generous and prudent parenthood. It does not then depend upon the direct fecundity of each and every particular act. Moreover the morality of every marital act depends upon the requirements of mutual love in all its aspects. In a word, the morality of sexual actions is thus to be judged by the true exigencies of the nature of human sexuality, whose meaning is maintained and promoted especially by conjugal chastity as we have said above.

More and more clearly, for a conscience correctly formed, a willingness to raise a family with full acceptance of the various human and Christian responsibilities is altogether distinguished from a mentality and way of married life which in its totality is egoistically and irrationally opposed to fruitfulness. This truly "contraceptive" mentality and practice has been condemned by the traditional doctrine of the church and will always be condemned as gravely sinful.

Chapter III: On the Continuity of Doctrine and its Deeper Understanding

The tradition of the church which is concerned with the morality of conjugal relations began with the beginning of the church. It should be observed, however, that the tradition developed in the argument and conflict with heretics such as the Gnostics, the Manichaeans and later the Cathari, all of whom condemned procreation or the transmission of life as something evil, and nonetheless indulged in moral vices. Consequently this tradition always, albeit with various words, intended to protect two fundamental values: the good of procreation and the rectitude of marital intercourse. Moreover the church always taught another truth equally fundamental, although hidden in a mystery, namely original sin. This had wounded man in his various faculties, including sexuality. Man could only be healed of this wound by the grace of a Saviour. This is one of the reasons why Christ took marriage and raised it to a sacrament of the New Law.

It is not surprising that in the course of centuries this tradition was always interpreted in expressions and formulas proper to the times and that the words with which it was expressed and the reasons on which it was based were changed by knowledge which is now obsolete. Nor was there maintained always a right equilibrium of all the elements. Some authors even used expressions which depreciated the matrimonial state. But what is of real importance is that the same values were again and again reaffirmed. Consequently an egotistical, hedonistic and contraceptive way which turns the practice of married life in an arbitrary fashion from its ordination to a human, generous and prudent fecundity is always against the nature of man and can never be justified.

The large amount of knowledge and facts which throw light on today's world suggest that it is not to contradict the genuine sense of this tradition and the purpose of the previous doctrinal condemnations if we speak of the regulation of conception by using means, human and decent, ordered to favoring fecundity in the totality of married life and toward the realization of the authentic values of a fruitful matrimonial community.

The reasons in favor of this affirmation are of several kinds: social changes in matrimony and the family, especially in the role of the woman; lowering of the infant mortality rate; new bodies of knowledge in biology, psychology, sexuality and demography; a changed estimation of the value and meaning of human sexuality and of conjugal relations; most of all, a better grasp of the duty of man to humanize and to bring to greater perfection for the life of man what is given in nature. Then must be considered the sense of the faithful: according to it, condemnation of a couple to a long and often heroic abstinence as the means to regulate conception, cannot be founded on the truth.

A further step in the doctrinal evolution, which it seems now should be developed, is founded less on these facts than on a better, deeper and more correct understanding of conjugal life and of the conjugal act when these other changes occur. The doctrine on marriage and its essential values remains the same and whole, but it is now applied differently out of a deeper understanding.

This maturation has been prepared and has already begun. The magisterium itself is in evolution. Leo XIII spoke less explicitly in his encyclical *Arcanum* than did Pius XI in his wonderful doctrinal synthesis of *Casti Connubii* of 1930 which gave a fresh start to so many beginnings in a living conjugal spirituality. He proclaimed, using the very words of the Roman Cate-chism, the importance, in a true sense the primary im-portance, of true conjugal love for the community of matrimony. The notion of responsible parenthood which is implied in the notion of a prudent and generous regulation of conception, advanced in Vatican Council II, had already been prepared by Pius XII. The ac-ceptance of a lawful application of the calculated sterile periods of the woman—that the application is legitimate presupposes right motives—makes a separation between the sexual act which is explicitly intended and its re-productive effect which is intentionally excluded.

The tradition has always rejected seeking this separa-tion with a contraceptive intention for motives spoiled by egoism and hedonism, and such seeking can never be admitted. The true opposition is not to be sought be-tween some material conformity to the physiological processes of nature and some artificial intervention. For it is natural to man to use his skill in order to put under human control what is given by physical nature. The opposition is really to be sought between one way of acting which is contraceptive and opposed to a pru-dent and generous fruitfulness, and another way which is in an ordered relationship to responsible fruitfulness and which has a concern for education and all the es-sential, human and Christian values.

In such a conception the substance of tradition stands in continuity and is respected. The new elements which today are discerned in tradition under the in-fluence of new knowledge and facts were found in it before; they were undifferentiated but not denied; so that the problem in today's terms is new and has not been proposed before in this way. In light of the new data these elements are being explained and made more precise. The moral obligation of following fundamental norms and fostering all the essential values in a balanced fashion is strengthened and not weakened. The virtue of chastity by which a couple positively regulates the practice of sexual relations is all the more demanded. The criteria of morality therefore which are human and Christian demand and at the same time foster a spirituality which is more profound in married life, with faith, hope and charity informed according to the spirit of the Gospel.

Chapter IV: The Objective Criteria of Morality

The question comes up which many men rightly think to be of great importance, at least practically: what are the objective criteria by which to choose a method of reconciling the needs of marital life with a right ordering of this life to fruitfulness in the procreation and education of offspring?

It is obvious that the method is not to be left to purely arbitrary decision.

(1) In resolving the similar problem of responsible parenthood and the appropriate determination of the size of the family, Vatican Council II has shown the way. The objective criteria are the various values and needs duly and harmoniously evaluated. These objective criteria are to be applied by the couples, acting from a rightly formed conscience and according to their concrete situation. In the words of the Council: "Thus they will fulfill their task with human and Christian responsibility. With docile reverence toward

God, they will come to the right decision by common
counsel and effort. They will thoughtfully take into account both their own welfare and that of their children,
those already born and those which may be foreseen.
For this accounting they will reckon with both the
material and spiritual conditions of the times as well
as of their state in life. Finally they will consult the
interests of the family community, of temporal society,
and of the church herself. . . . But in their manner of
acting, spouses should be aware that they cannot proceed arbitrarily. They must always be governed according to a conscience dutifully conformed to the Divine
Law itself, and should be submissive toward the church's
teaching office, which authentically interprets that law
in the light of the Gospel" (*Constitution on the Church
in the Modern World,* II, c.1, par.50; cf c.5, par.87).

In other questions of conjugal life, one should proceed in the same way. There are various objective
criteria which are concretely applied by couples themselves acting with a rightly formed conscience. All, for
an example, know that objective criteria prohibit that
the intimate acts of conjugal life, even if carried out in
a way which could be called "natural," be practiced if
there is a loss of physical or psychic health or if there
is neglect of the personal dignity of the spouses or if
they are carried out in an egoistic or hedonistic way.
These objective criteria are the couples', to be applied
by them to their concrete situation, avoiding pure
arbitrariness in forming their judgment. It is impossible
to determine exhaustively by a general judgment and
ahead of time for each individual case what these objective criteria will demand in the concrete situation
of a couple.

(2) Likewise, there are objective criteria as to the means to be chosen of responsibly determining the size of the family: If they are rightly applied, the couples themselves will find and determine the way of proceeding.

In grave language, Vatican Council II has reaffirmed that abortion is altogether to be excluded from the means of responsibly preventing birth. Indeed, abortion is not a method of preventing conception but of eliminating offspring already conceived. This affirmation about acts which do not spare an offspring already conceived is to be repeated in regard to those interventions as to which there is serious grounds to suspect that they are abortive.

Sterilization, since it is a drastic and irreversible intervention in a matter of great importance, is generally to be excluded as a means of responsibly avoiding conceptions.

Moreover, the natural law and reason illuminated by Christian faith dictate that a couple proceed in choosing means not arbitrarily but according to objective criteria. These objective criteria for the right choice of methods are the conditions for keeping and fostering the essential values of marriage as a community of fruitful love. If these criteria are observed, then a right ordering of the human act according to its object, end and circumstances is maintained.

Among these criteria, this must be put first: the action must correspond to the nature of the person and of his acts so that the whole meaning of the mutual giving and of human procreation is kept in a context of true love (cf. *Constitution on the Church in the Modern World*, II, c.1, par.51). *Secondly,* the means which are chosen should have an effectiveness proportionate to the degree of right or necessity of averting a new conception temporarily or permanently. *Thirdly,* every method of preventing conception—not excluding either periodic or absolute abstinence—carries with it some negative element or physical evil which the couple more or less seriously feels. This negative element or physical evil can arise under different aspects: account must be taken of the biological, hygienic, and psychological aspects, the personal dignity of the spouses, and the possibility of expressing sufficiently and aptly the interpersonal relation or conjugal love. The means to be chosen, where several are possible, is that which carries with it the least possible negative element, according to the concrete situation of the couple. *Fourthly,* then, in choosing concretely among means, much depends on what means may be available in a certain region or at a certain time or for a certain couple; and this may depend on the economic situation.

Therefore not arbitrarily, but as the law of nature and of God commands, let couples form a judgment which is objectively founded, with all the criteria considered. This they may do without major difficulty, and with peace of mind, if they take common and prudent counsel before God. They should, however, to the extent possible, be instructed about the criteria by competent persons and be educated as to the right application of the criteria. Well instructed, and prudently educated as Christians, they will prudently and serenely decide what is truly for the good of the couple and of the children, and does not neglect their own personal Christian perfection, and is, therefore, what God revealing himself through the natural law and Christian revelation, sets before them to do.

Chapter I: The Task and Fundamental Conditions of Educational Renewal

When sometimes a new aspect of human life obtains a special place in the area of man's responsibility, a task of educational renewal is imposed in a seriously binding way.

In order that spouses may take up the duty of responsible parenthood, they must grasp, more than in the past, the meaning of fruitfulness and experience a desire for it. In order that they may give to married life its unitive value, and do so in service of its procreative function, they must develop an increasingly purer respect for their mutual needs, the sense of community and the acceptance of their common Christian vocation.

It will not be a surprise that this conviction of a greater responsibility will come about as the effect and crown of a gradual development of the meaning of marriage and conjugal spirituality. For several generations, in an always increasing number, couples have sought to live their proper married vocation in a more profound and more conscientious way. The doctrine of the magisterium and especially the encyclical *Casti Connubii* notably contributed and strengthened this formation of conscience by giving to it its full meaning.

The more urgent the appeal is made to observe mutual love and charity in every expression of married life, the more urgent is the necessity of forming consciences, of educating spouses to a sense of responsibility and of awakening a right sense of values. This new step in the development of conjugal life cannot bear all its fruits, unless it is accompanied by an immense educational activity. No one will regret that these new demands stirred by the Holy Spirit call the entire human race to this profound moral maturity.

Couples who might think they find in the doctrine as it has just been proposed an open door to laxism or easy solutions make a grave mistake, of which they will be the first victims. The conscientious decision to be made by spouses about the number of children is not a matter of small importance. On the contrary it imposes a more conscientious fulfilling of their vocation to fruitfulness in the consideration of a whole complex of values which are involved here. The same is true of the responsibility of the spouses for the development of their common life in such a way that it will be a source of continual progress and perfection.

The God who created man male and female, in order that they might be two in one flesh, in order that they might bring the world under their control, in order that they might increase and multiply (Gen. 1–2), is the God who has elevated their union to the dignity of a sacrament and so disposed that in this world it is a special sign of His own love for His people. He Himself will gird the spouses with His strength, His light, His love and His joy in the strength of the spirit of Christ. Who then would doubt that couples, all couples, will not be able to respond to the demands of their vocation?

Chapter II: Further Consideration;
Application of the Doctrine of Matrimony to
Different Parts of the World

(1) It seems very necessary to establish some pontifical institute or secretariat for the study of the sciences connected with married life. In this commission there could be continual collaboration in open dialogue among experts competent in various areas. The aim of this institute (or secretariat) would be, among other duties, to carry further the research and reflection begun by the commission. The various studies which the commission has already done could be made public. It would be in a special way for this institute to study how the doctrine of matrimony should be applied to different parts of the world and to contribute to the formation of priests and married couples dedicated to the family apostolate by sending experts to them (cf., *Constitution on the Church in the Modern World,* II, c.1, par.52).

(2) Universal principles and the essential values of matrimony and married life become actual in ways which partially differ according to different cultures and different mentalities. Consequently there is a special task for episcopal conferences to institute organizations for investigation and dialogue between families, between representatives of the different sciences and pastors of souls. They would also have the task of judging which may be in practice the more apt pastoral means in each region to promote the healthy formation of consciences and education to a sense of responsibility.

Episcopal conferences should be particularly concerned that priests and married lay persons be adequately formed in a more spiritual and moral understanding of Christian matrimony. Thus they will be prepared to extend pastoral action to the renewal of families in the spirit of *"aggiornamento"* initiated by the *Constitution on the Church in the Modern World.*

Under their guidance there should also be action to start in each region the genuine fostering of all families in the context of social evolution which should be truly human. The fostering of the role of woman is of special importance here.

There are many reforms and initiatives which are needed to open the way to decent and joyful living for all families. Together with all men of good will, Christians must approach this great work of human development, without which the elevation of families can never become actual. Christianity does not teach some ideal for a small number of elect, but the vocation of all to the essential values of human life. It cannot be that anyone would wish to elevate his own family without at the same time actively dedicating himself to opening a way for similar elevation for all families in all parts of the world.

Chapter III: Demographic Facts and Policy

The increase of inhabitants cannot in any way be said to be something evil or calamitous for the human race. As children are "the most excellent gift of matrimony" (*Constitution on the Church in the Modern World,* II, c.I, par.50) and the object of the loving care of the parents, which demands from them many sacrifices, so the great number of men pertaining to a certain nation and constituting the whole human race spread over the globe is the foundation of all social sharing and cultural progress. Thus there should be afforded to it all those things which according to social justice are due to men as persons.

The Church is not ignorant of the immense difficulties and profound transformations which have arisen from the conditions of contemporary life throughout the world and especially in certain regions where there has been a rapid rise in population. That is why she again and again raises her voice to urge various nations and the whole human family to help one another in truly human progress, united in true solidarity and excluding every intention of domination. Then they might avoid all those things both in the political and in the social order which restrict or dissipate in an egotistical way the full utilization of the goods of the earth which are destined for all men.

The Church by her doctrine and by her supernatural aids intends to help all families so that they might find the right way in undertaking their generous and prudent responsibility. Governments which have the care of the common good should look with great concern on sub-human conditions of families and "beware of solutions contradicting the moral law, solutions which have been promoted publicly or privately, and sometimes actually imposed" (*Constitution on the Church in the Modern World,* II, c.5, par.87). These solutions have contradicted the moral law in particular by propagating abortion or sterilization. Political demography can be called human only if the rights of parents with regard to the procreation and education of children are respected and conditions of life are fostered with all vigor so that parents are enabled to exercise their responsibilities before God and society.

Chapter IV: The Inauguration and
Further Development of Means for Education
of Couples and Youth

(1) Couples are burdened by multiple responsibilities throughout the whole of life; they seek light and aid. With the favor of God there will develop in many regions what has already been initiated often by the married couples themselves, to sustain families in their building and continual development.

Maximum help is to be given to parents in their educational task. They strongly desire to provide the best for their children. The more parents are conscious of their office of fruitfulness, which is extended over the whole time in which the education of their children is accomplished, so much the more do they seek a way of acquiring better preparation to carry out this responsibility. Moreover, in exercising this educational office, the spouses mature more deeply in it themselves, create a unity, become rich in love, and apply themselves with the high task of giving themselves with united energies to the high task of giving life and education.

(2) The building up of the conjugal and family community does not happen without thought. Therefore it is fitting everywhere to set up and work out many better means of remote and immediate preparation of youth for marriage. This requires the collaboration of everyone. Married people who are already well educated will have a great and indispensable part in this work. In these tasks of providing help to spouses and to the young who are preparing to build and develop a conjugal and family community, priests and religious will cooperate closely with the families. Without this cooperation, in which each one has his own indispensa-

ble part, there will never be apt methods of education to those responsibilities of the vocation which places the sacrament in clear light so that its full and profound meaning shines forth.

The Church, which holds the deposit of the gospel, has to bring this noble message to all men in the entire world. This announcing of the gospel, grounded in love, illumines every aspect of married and family life. Every aspect, every task and responsibility of the conjugal and family community shines with a clear light, in love toward one's neighbor—a love which is rich with human values and is formed by the divine interpersonal love of Father, Son and Holy Spirit. May the spirit of Christ's love more and more penetrate families everywhere so that together with John, the beloved disciple of Jesus, married couples, parents and children may always understand more deeply the wonderful relation between love of God and love of one another (I John 4: 7–5, 4).

13

Minority Papal Commission Report *

———◆◆◆———

The document published here presents the views of the conservative minority among the theologians who took part in the final session of the papal birth control meeting last spring. It is the longest of the three major papers and was described by N.C.R.'s translators as the most difficult to interpret. Its authors are Father John Ford, U.S. Jesuit on the faculty of the Catholic University, Washington; Father Jan Visser, Dutch Redemptorist who is rector of St. Alphonsus college, Rome; the Rev. Marcelino Zalba, Spanish Jesuit, a teacher of moral theology at the Gregorian University, Rome; and Father Stanley de Lestapis, S.J., sociologist and author, Vanves, France.

* From *National Catholic Reporter*, April 19, 1967.

A. The State of the Question

The central question to which the Church must now respond is this: *Is contraception always seriously evil?* All other questions discussed are reduced in the final analysis to this simple and central question. If a clear answer is given to this question, other questions can be solved without great theological difficulty. The whole world, the faithful as well as the non-believers, wish to know what the Church will now have to say on this question.

Contraception is understood by the Church as any use of the marriage right in the exercise of which the act is deprived of its natural power for the procreation of life through the industry of men. *Contraceptive sterilization* is related to the definition of contraception just given. It may be defined theologically as any physical intervention in the generative process (*opus naturae*) which, before or after the proper placing of generative acts (*opus hominis*), causes these acts to be deprived of their natural power for the procreation of life by the industry of man.

Always evil. Something which can never be justified by any motive or any circumstance is always evil because it is intrinsically evil. It is wrong not because of a precept of positive law, but of reason of the natural law. It is not evil because it is prohibited, but it is prohibited because it is evil. Homicide may be used as an example, inasmuch as the direct killing of an innocent person can be justified by no motive and no circumstance whatsoever. Understanding "something which is always evil" in this sense, the faithful are now asking the Church: is contraception always seriously evil?

B. What Answer Has the Church Given to This Question up to Now?

A constant and perennial affirmative answer is found in the documents of the magisterium and in the whole history of teaching on the question.

(1) First of all, some more recent documents of the pontifical teaching authority may be cited, namely, the encyclical *Casti Connubii* of Pius XI (1930); the *Allocution to Midwives* of Pius XII (1951); the encyclical *Mater et Magistra* of John XXIII (1961).

Pius XI, *Casti Connubii* (par.54, 56, 57):

But no reason, however grave, may be put forward by which anything *intrinsically* against nature may become conformable to nature and morally good. Since, therefore, *the conjugal act* is destined primarily *by nature* for the begetting of children, those who in exercising it deliberately frustrate its natural power and purpose sin against nature and commit a deed which is shameful and *intrinsically vicious* . . .

Since, therefore, openly departing from the *uninterrupted Christian tradition* some recently have judged it possible solemnly to declare another doctrine regarding this question, the Catholic Church, to whom God has entrusted the defense of the integrity and purity of morals, standing erect in the midst of the moral ruin which surrounds her, in order that she may *preserve the chastity of the nuptial union from being defiled by this foul stain,* raises her voice in token of her divine ambassadorship and *through our mouth proclaims anew: any use whatsoever of matrimony exercised in such a way that the act is deliberately frustrated in its natural power to generate life is an offense against the law of God and of nature,* and those who indulge in such are branded with the guilts of a grave sin . . .

If any confessor or pastor of souls, which may God forbid, leads the faithful entrusted to him into these errors or should at least confirm them by approval or by guilty silence, let him be mindful of the fact that he must render a strict account to God, the Supreme Judge, for the betrayal of his sacred trust, and let him take to himself the words of Christ: "They are blind and leaders of the blind: and if the blind lead the blind, both fall into the pit."

Pius XII, *Allocution to Midwives,* 1951:

In his Encyclical *Casti Connubii* of Dec. 31, 1930, our prodecessor, Pius XII, of happy memory, solemnly restated the basic law of the conjugal act and conjugal relations. "Every attempt on the part of the married couple during the conjugal act or during the development of its natural consequences, to deprive it of its inherent power and to hinder the procreation of a new life is immoral. No 'indication' or need can change an action that is intrinsically immoral into an action that is moral and lawful."

This prescription holds good today just as much as it did yesterday. It will hold tomorrow and always, for it is not a mere precept of human right but the expression of a natural and Divine Law . . .

Let our words be for you equivalent to a sure norm in all those things in which your profession and apostolic task demands that you work with a certain and firm opinion . . .

Direct sterilization, that which aims at making procreation impossible as both means and end, is a grave violation of the moral law, and therefore illicit. Even public authority has no right to permit it under the pretext of any "indication" whatsover, and still less to prescribe it, or to have it carried out to the harm of the innocent . . .

Other addresses of Pius XII should be noted in which till the end of his life he explicitly and implicitly reiterated that contraception was always gravely evil. Note, for example, his address to the Roman Rota (1941); to Catholic doctors (1949); to families (1951); to histopathologists (1952); to the Society of Urologists (1953); to a symposium of geneticists (1953); to the

Congress for Fertility and Sterility (1956); to the Society of Hematologists (1958).

John XXIII, *Mater et Magistra,* 1961, writes as follows:

Hence, the real solution of the problem (over-population) is not to be found in expedients which offend against the divinely established moral order or which attack human life at its very source, but in a renewed, scientific and technical effort on man's part to deepen and extend his dominion over nature . . . The transmission of human life is the result of a personal and conscious act, and, as such, is subject to the all-holy, inviolable and immutable laws of God, which no man may ignore or disobey. He is not therefore, permitted to use certain ways and means which are allowable in the propagation of plant and animal life. Human life is sacred—all men must recognize that fact. From its inception it reveals the creating hand of God. Those who violate his laws not only offend the Divine Majesty and degrade themselves and humanity, they also sap the vitality of the political community of which they are the members. (par. 189, 193, 194).

(2) The answer of the Church in the present century is also illustrated by *declarations of the bishops* either (a) *collectively* speaking in a particular region or (b) speaking *individually* in their own diocese.

(a) The German bishops, 1913, (and from this followed their "Instruction for Confessors" several years later); the French bishops, 1919; the bishops of the United States of America, 1920; the Belgian bishops, 1920; the bishops of India, 1960; the bishops of the United States of America, 1959; the bishops of England, 1964; the bishops of Honduras, 1966. In Spain, 1919, there were eight dioceses in which conjugal onanism was a reserved sin.

(b) Here are several examples of pastoral letters of this century; Rutten, Liege, 1907; Mercier, Malines, 1909; Cologne, 1913; Cardinal Bourne, Westminster, 1930; Cardinal Montini, Milan, 1960; Cardinal Gracias, Bombay, 1961. More notable was the declaration of Cardinal Bourne, immediately after the Lambeth Conference of 1930, because of the fact that he publicly denounced the (Anglican) bishops of the Lambeth Conference as if they had abdicated all title whereby they could pretend to be "authoritative interpreters of Christian morality."

It must be noted that the Holy See between 1816 and 1929, through the Roman curia, answered questions in this matter 19 times. Since then it has spoken almost as many times. In the responses given, it was at least implicitly supposed that contraception was always seriously evil.

(3) History provides fullest evidence (cf. especially the excellent work of Professor John T. Noonan, *Contraception,* Harvard University Press, 1965) that the answer of the Church has always and everywhere been the same, from the beginning up to the present decade. One can find no period of history, no document of the church, no theological school, scarcely one Catholic theologian, who ever denied that contraception was always seriously evil. The teaching of the Church in this matter is absolutely constant. Until the present century this teaching was peacefully possessed by all other Christians, whether Orthodox or Anglican or Protestant. The Orthodox retain this as common teaching today.

The theological history of the use of matrimony is very complicated. It evolved very much in the course of the centuries up to the Second Vatican Council.

Teachings which have slowly evolved this way are especially: concerning the nature of sexual concupiscence; the teaching of the malice (venial) of the use of matrimony without the procreative intention or from motives of concupiscence; the teaching about the positive value of the sexual element in the use of matrimony, and as it involves conjugal love. Then too, human sexuality and its genuine value is now being treated more positively. The history of this evolution is by no means simple.

On the contrary, the theological history of contraception, comparatively speaking, is sufficiently simple, at least with regard to the central question: Is contraception always seriously evil? For in answer to this question there has never been any variation and scarcely any evolution in the teaching. The ways of formulating and explaining this teaching have evolved, but not the doctrine itself.

Therefore it is not a question of a teaching proposed in 1930 which because of new physiological facts and new theological perspectives ought to be changed. It is a question rather of a teaching which until the present decade was constantly and authentically taught by the Church.

C. Unsatisfactory Explanations of the Origin and Evolution of the Church's Teaching

Among those who wish to change the doctrine (or who declare that it has already evolved), are those who appeal to various past circumstances, as if the malice of contraception was rooted in these circumstances and was to be explained by them. Further, they argue that since these circumstances have entirely changed, the teaching itself can legitimately be changed. Examples of this kind of argumentation follow.

(1) Some say that the foundation of this teaching was the following biblical text: "increase and multiply." The malice of contraception would then be in the violation of this affirmative precept, But theologians and the Church have considered contraception as a violation not of an affirmative precept, but of a negative precept which obliges always and everywhere: "Let no one impede human life in its proximate causes," or "let no one violate the ordination of this act and processes to the good of the species."

Theologians have never said "Homicide is always evil because God has said, 'Increase and multiply'; but because He has said, 'You may not kill the innocent.' " Similarly they have not said that contraception is evil because God has said, "Increase and multiply"; but because they have considered it in some way analogous to homicide. This analogy was constant in tradition up until the eighteenth century and still more recently it was invoked by the hierarchy of Germany (1913) and India (1960). Through the course of the centuries the malice of contraception has lain in the violation of the essential ordination of the generative faculty to the good of the species. It has been expressed in various formulations. But in every age it is clearly evident that contraception especially offends against the negative percept: "One may not deprive the conjugal act of its natural power for the procreation of new life."

(2) Some say that the Church condemned contraception because of demographic needs, the necessity among rural people for larger families, the high mortality rate among the newborn, etc. So they argue, since

these situations no longer exist, the foundation of the teaching has been removed and the teaching itself ought to be set aside.

As an answer to this, it must be said that both St. Augustine and St. Thomas taught that our earth was already sufficiently populated. There is no proof that such considerations as those cited in this paragraph have had any effect on the teaching of the Fathers, or theologians, or the magisterium.

(3) Some say that older theologians had prohibited contraception because they falsely supposed that the procreative intention is always required in order that the use of matrimonial rights might not be considered sinful. In answer: clearly the necessity of procreative intention was regularly insisted upon, lest there be committed a *venial* sin of sexual concupiscence, and without a doubt this teaching confirmed the condemnation of contraception. But is is impossible to understand how the *serious evil* of contraception could then be cited as an *insignificant* failure in the matter of chastity. Among theologians contraception was a damnable vice, an anticipated homicide, a serious and unnatural sin. Now to explain its malice by appealing to a defect in the procreative intention would be as inept as to say that a murderer merits capital punishment *because* he used another's instrument without permission in committing the homicide. It is not the teaching concerning the malice of contraception which has evolved now but rather the teaching of sexual concupiscence in the use of matrimony.

(4) Some say that the teaching of the Church was founded on the false supposition that all conjugal acts are procreative by their very nature, whereas the facts

of physiology show that very few of them are actually fertile or productive of new life. In answer to this, it must be said that the older thinkers knew that many conjugal acts are actually sterile, e.g., during pregnancy and old age. Moreover, a legitimate conclusion from the facts now known would be this: there are fewer acts which are as a matter of fact capable of producing new life; therefore, there are fewer acts against which a person in acting contraceptively would incur the specific malice of contraception. But the facts do not invite us to intervene contraceptively, now that we have a more accurate knowledge about fertility; rather they invite us to have a greater respect for them.

(5) Others say that the teaching of the Church is based on an obsolete medieval notion of "nature," according to which nature would order its own processes to its own natural ends, fixed by the "intention of nature," and of God. Contraception, as something going against the order established by nature, would be considered intrinsically evil because it is "contrary to nature."

In answer to this: the teaching of the Church was first fully formulated and handed down constantly for several centuries before scholastic philosophy was refined. Secondly, in no way does it derive from any philosophy of nature (of the scholastics, stoics or others) in which the natural physical order is the *general criterion* of morality for man. Thirdly, theology (just as scholastic philosophy) does not say that the physical ordering of things to their natural end is inviolable with respect to being "natural." It does attribute a special inviolability to this act and to the generative process precisely because they are generative of new *human life,* and life is not under man's dominion. It is not because of some philosophy which would make the physical order of nature as such the criterion of the morality of human acts.

D. Why Does the Church Teach that Contraception Is Always Seriously Evil?

If we could bring forward arguments which are clear and cogent based on reason alone, it would not be necessary for our commission to exist, nor would the present state of affairs exist in the Church as it is.

(1) The fathers, theologians, and the Church herself has always taught that certain acts and the generative processes are in some way specially inviolable precisely because they are generative. This inviolability is always attributed to the act and to the process, which are biological; not inasmuch as they are biological, but inasmuch as they are human, namely inasmuch as they are the object of *human acts* and are destined by their nature to the good of the human species.

(2) This inviolability was explained for many centuries by the Fathers, the theologians and in canon law as analogous to the inviolability of human life itself. This analogy is not merely rhetorical or metaphorical, but it expressed a fundamental moral truth. Human life already existing *(in facto esse)* is inviolable. Likewise, it is also in some sense inviolable in its proximate causes *(vita in fieri)*. To put it in another way: just as already existing human life is removed from the dominion of man, so also in some similar way is human life as it comes to be; that is, the act and the generative process, inasmuch as they are generative, are removed from his dominion. In the course of centuries, scholastic philosophy explained this inviolability further and grounded it in the essential ordination of the act and the generative process to the good of the species.

(3) The substratum of this teaching would seem to presuppose various Christian conceptions concerning the nature of God and of man, the union of the soul and the body which creates *one* human person, God as the Supreme Lord of human life, the special creation of each individual human soul. Moreover, the value of human life is presupposed as a fundamental good, which has in itself the reason for its inviolability, not because it is of man but because it is of God. This quasi-sacredness of natural human life (recall the quotation from John XXIII) is extended in the teaching of the Church to the acts and generative processes in as much as they are such. At least this is the way the matter must be conceived if we wish to understand the ancient traditional analogy to homicide and the severity with which the Fathers, the theologians and all faithful Christians have constantly rejected contraception.

Nor should one exclude from his view that malice in contraception which is derived precisely from violated chastity: first, because chastity is understood as regulating the total generative process; and secondly, because (especially in antiquity) the conjugal act which proceeded from unexcused concupiscence was considered for this reason to be venially sinful.

(4) The philosophical arguments by which the teaching of the Church is attacked are diversely proposed by diverse people. Some see the malice principally in the fact that procreation itself (that is, the act and the generative process) is a certain fundamental human good (as truth, as life itself is such a good). To destroy

it voluntarily is therefore evidently evil. For to have an intention, directly and actively contrary to a fundamental human good, is something intrinsically evil. St. Thomas spoke of this good, in discussing the matter, referring to "man in his proximate potency."

Others derive its malice also from the disorientation whereby the act and the process, which are destined for the good of the species, are essentially deprived of their relation to this good of the species, and are subordinated to the good of the individual. Pius XII developed this argument.

(5) But note: First, the question is not merely or principally philosophical. It depends on the nature of human life and human sexuality, as understood theologically by the Church. Secondly, in this matter men need the help of the teaching of the Church, explained and applied under the leadership of the magisterium, so that they can with certitude and security embrace the way, the truth and the life.

Pius XI spoke to the point in *Casti Connubii:*

But everyone can see to how many fallacies an avenue would be opened up and how many errors would become mixed with the truth, if it were left solely to the light of reason of each to find it out, or if it were to be discovered by the private interpretation of the truth which is revealed. And if this is applicable to many other truths of moral order, we must all the more pay attention to those things which appertain to marriage where the inordinate desire for pleasure can attack frail human nature and easily deceive it and lead it astray . . .

For Christ Himself made the Church the teacher of truth in those things also which concern the right regulation of moral conduct, even though some knowledge of the same is not beyond human reason.

E. Why Cannot the Church Change Her Answer to This Central Question?

(1) The Church cannot change her answer *because this answer is true*. Whatever may pertain to a more perfect formulation of the teaching or its possible genuine development, the teaching itself cannot not be substantially true. It is true because the Catholic Church, instituted by Christ to show men a secure way to eternal life, could not have so wrongly erred during all those centuries of its history. The Church cannot substantially err in teaching doctrine which is most serious in its import for faith and morals, throughout all centuries or even one century, if it has been constantly and forcefully proposed as necessarily to be followed in order to obtain eternal salvation. The Church could not have erred through so many centuries, even through one century, by imposing under serious obligation very grave burdens in the name of Jesus Christ, if Jesus Christ did not actually impose these burdens. The Catholic Church could not have furnished in the name of Jesus Christ to so many of the faithful everywhere in the world, through so many centuries, the occasion for formal sin and spiritual ruin, because of a false doctrine promulgated in the name of Jesus Christ.

If the Church could err in such a way, the authority of the ordinary magisterium in moral matters would be thrown into question. The faithful could not put their trust in the magisterium's presentation of moral teaching, especially in sexual matters.

(2) *Our question is not about the irreformability of Casti Connubii*. The teaching of the Church did not have its beginning in *Casti Connubii,* nor does it depend on the precise degree of authority with which Pius XI wished to teach the Church in that document. The teaching of the Church in this matter would have its own validity and truth even if *Casti Connubii* had never been written. (When it was published, all saw in it not something new but the true teaching of the Church.) Our question is a question of the *truth* of this proposition: contraception is always seriously evil. The truth of this teaching stems from the fact that it has been proposed with such constancy, with such universality, with such obligatory force, always and everywhere, as something to be held and followed by the faithful. Technical and juridical investigation into the irreformability and infallibility of *Casti Connubii* (as if once this obstacle had been removed, the true doctrine could be found and taught) distracts from the central question and even prejudices the question.

(3) One can subtly dispute about many questions: e.g., whether the teaching is infallible by reason of the wording of *Casti Connubii;* whether the Church can teach something infallibly or define what is not formally revealed; whether the Church can teach authoritatively and in an obligatory fashion the principles of the natural law, whether infallible or not. But after all this, in practice we know what the Church can do from the things which she has always done, either implicitly by some action, or explicitly by invoking her power, derived from Christ Himself, of teaching the faithful in moral matters.

In dealing with this question, to dispute in a subtle way whether the teaching is technically "infallible by a judgment of the magisterium" is empty-headed *(supervacaneum).* For if this doctrine is not substantially true, the magisterium itself will seem to be empty and useless in any moral matter.

F. New Notions of the Magisterium
and Its Authority

(1) What has been commonly held and handed down concerning the nature, function and authority of the magisterium does not seem to be accepted by everyone today. For among those who say that the teaching of *Casti Connubii* is reformable and who say that contraception is not always intrinsically evil, some seem to have a concept which is radically different about the nature and function of the magisterium, especially in moral matters. Thus, in the report of our commission's general session (plenary), March 25–28, 1965, pages 52–53, we read the following presentation of certain members' opinions:

I. Nature is not something totally complete, but is in some sense "making itself." We cannot attain it except by taking an overall view, because a fixed concept of nature does not exist . . .

II. The principle of continuity does not refer to precise judgments about the manner of acting (*"comportements"*) as if they were once and for all determined for everyone. Rather it refers to the permanent values which must be protected, discovered and realized. Consequently, continuity refers neither to the formulations nor to concrete solutions. It suffices in a particular moment if the judgment on a moral matter is true "for the moment," (*geschichtsgerecht*, historically valid) . . .

IV. The function of the magisterium, therefore, does not consist in defining ways of acting (*"comportements"*) in moral matters, unless one is speaking of prudential guidance. For its proper role, as for the Gospel, is to provide those broader clarifications which are needed. But it could

not publish edicts of such a nature that they would bind
consciences to precise ways of acting; that would be to proceed against that respect for life which is an absolute
value . . .

It is no surprise, then, if theologians in the contemporary Church have no difficulty either in acknowledg-
ing the Church to have erred or in explaining what now
they call erroneous as something historically true and
valid for the time in which it took place, or even in
denying to the magisterium of the Church the power
of binding the consciences of the faithful in current
concrete cases, especially touching on the question of
natural law.

(2) Those who proceed along the more traditional
way in this matter cite various documents of the Holy
See. Here are a few examples:

(a) Pius XII in his address *Magnificate Dominum*
(1954):

The power of the Church is never limited to matters of
"strictly religious concern," as they say. Rather the entire
matter of the natural law, its institutions, interpretation,
application, inasmuch as it is a question of moral concern,
are in her power. For the observance of the natural law
out of respect for the ordination of God looks to the way
by which man must move along to his final supernatural
end. The Church is already in this way the guardian and
leader of men toward his end which is above nature. The
Church, from the Apostles down to our times, has always
maintained this manner of acting and will today, not just
by way of guide and private council, but by the mandate
and authority of the Lord.

(b) John XXIII, in his encyclical *Peace on Earth*

(1963), where he is speaking of social matters and the authority of the Church to apply the principles of the natural law:

Let no one object to the fact that it is the right and duty of the Church, not only to safeguard the teaching of faith and morals, but also to interpose her authority among her sons in the area of external affairs, when it is necessary to determine how that teaching may be made effective.

(c) The Second Vatican Council, in the *Constitution on the Church in the Modern World,* no. 25, reaffirms the obligatory character of the teaching authority of the supreme pontiff when he teaches authentically, even if not infallibly.

Furthermore, among those who think that the Church today can now say "contraception is not seriously evil," there seem to be some who conceive human nature as something continually and essentially evolving. There are some who will admit no intrinsic evil as necessarily connected with any external human action. There are some who permit suicide, abortion, fornication and even adultery in certain circumstances. There are some who, equivalently at least in these matters, defend the principle that the end justifies the means. There are some who promote situation morality, and a morality of relativism, or the "new morality." There are some who deny or doubt that the teaching authority of the Church can teach moral truth of the natural law infallibly. There are some who seem to deny that the teaching authority of the Church can oblige the consciences of the faithful in a concrete and individual case in any moral matter. The conclusions in our area of interest, derived from such principles, must be examined ac-

curately, so that we may see to what further conclusions they will finally push us.

G. A Brief Summary of Recent
Doctrinal Development

(1) With regard to sexual acts and their natural consequences, it is possible to do the following:

(a) practice *continence;*

(b) an imperfect or incomplete act, including *am-
plexus reservatus;*

(c) intervene in the *operation of nature without a
mutilation,* for example, by using the pill for contraception;

(d) intervene in the *operation of nature by a irreversible surgery,* for instance, through sterilization;

(e) intervene in *man's operation (opus hominis),* by
depriving the act itself of procreative power, as through
onanism;

(f) intervene against the embryo, considering it not
yet animated by a rational soul;

(g) intervene against the fetus, animated by a rational soul, by abortion properly so-called;

(h) intervene against a newly born deformed child.

(2) Interventions (a) to (d) do not corrupt the act
in itself; (c) and (d) intervene in the natural operation
(opus naturae), but before the beginning *of any kind* of
new life. Intervention (e) has to do with *man's operation (opus hominis),* namely, through onanism which is
against the operation of the spermata. Interventions (f)
and (g) touch on the *fertilized ovum.* The medieval
doubt now reappears when a person asks whether it is
animated by a rational soul at the moment of fertiliza-

tion or later; or perhaps when the differentiation of the placenta and the embryo begins after nidation.

(3) Until now the Church has condemned human interventions in genital activity from (c) on, whether it was a question of impeding or frustrating the natural power of conjugal intercourse. After a few years, some theologians allowed intervention (c). Then some allowed (d) for special cases. Many with ease allow even (e) at least when it is not a question of a condom impeding intimate union. Some seem prepared to admit (f) if it can be established with certainty that the rational soul does not come into existence at the moment of fertilization. Further it would seem that (g) is *not absolutely* excluded by all. And indeed, this seems logical. On that account, there should be a careful indication of the previous steps just described.

PHILOSOPHICAL FOUNDATIONS AND ARGUMENTS OF OTHERS AND CRITIQUE

*(Not all approved everything,
or proposed things in the same way.)*

A. Synthetic Presentation

(1) The *immutable principles of the natural law seem to come down to:*

(a) subjection to God;

(b) reverence for the human person—often only in its spiritual element, and in a partial fashion;

(c) the duty of promoting earthly culture by humanizing nature.

When these values are preserved, man's intervention

in nature is not limited *a priori* by any absolute boundaries. This holds for one's own organism, when all superstitious reverence for biological integrity has been eliminated. Parts, organs, functions of man are conceived as contra-distinct from him. They are subordinated to him because of cultural values, almost as are plants and animals. So now they approve masturbation as being useful therapeutically; sterilization to avoid danger to life from use of the genital function in marriage; and action taken against the fetus so that at least the one giving birth will live. Their *basic reasoning:* in the complexity of these interventions, true existential values are sought through the best method available at the time.

(2) *Human nature and the particular norms of morality* are conceived of as adaptable and perfectible historically, so that they admit of *true changes.* They do not mean merely new applications and new modes of proceeding where the natural quality of such actions may depend on extrinsic conditions. Then, when man's fecundity and mortality have been modified, his sexual activity ought not to be changed, but rather the moral norm laid down for it in *Casti Cannubii,* by taking away natural procreativity from generative acts. To the extent that this frustration affords personal utility, it bestows value and is considered rightly ordered.

(3) *The teaching authority of the Church ought not to impede the development of culture* by limiting the control of nature or by defining methods of action. Experience will show what is good, or what is evil, in the concrete situations, as the experiencing subject here and now discovers. So then, (a) the magisterium, taught by

the experience of past errors, may not propose as infallible whatever is not clearly in revelation; (b) conscious of its limitations, it will not impose as the norm of the natural law what the greater number of the faithful sense as uncertain but it will dictate reasonable criteria for a given time (this is the way to interpret the declaration of *Casti Connubii*). These criteria are changeable and should be changed according to the progress of culture; (c) in the study of nature the magisterium will leave methods of action up to the discretion and responsibility of scientists, by not impeding the investigation of Catholics as it has often done in the past, with the loss of some influence in the world. ("Methods" they understand not merely in their technical aspect, but inasmuch as science show them to be more apt for humanitarian ends, and thus moralizes them through the intention, for example, as it moralizes conception by ordering it to the regulation of births.)

(4) *As moral criteria of the methods for exploring nature,* for bettering them and making them more humane, the following should be considered:

(a) the basic intention of the person acting, which must be worthy of man and enriching his values. This is to be considered in the total complex of his action—not necessarily in single actions, standing by themselves, but subordinated to a higher finality.

(b) The means to accomplish this are not to harm immediately the dignity or the rights of others, that is, they are not to use others as a means to bring about what they value. Otherwise means are morally indifferent and are to be specified by the intention of the person acting.

(c) Damage which might be caused by physical necessity in interventions whose effects can be known and decided in advance should be as minimal as possible.

(d) That method of action should be used which is the more humanitarian for a given situation.

(5) *The significance and morality of sexuality in marriage.*

(I) The following points, acknowledged by everyone, do not enter into the present discussion:

(a) the importance of sexuality for the perfecting and ordering of human existence, inasmuch as it is sexual;

(b) the dignity of conjugal love and its beneficial influence on the procreative society;

(c) the fittingness and definite moral necessity of more frequent carnal acts for couples to keep up their conjugal harmony and enthusiasm for having and educating offspring;

(d) the nobility of this act, holding a mean between its contemporary exaltation and the pessimistic evaluation of it in the past;

(e) the obligation of responsible paternity, attentive to the future education of children according to the condition of the family and of society;

(f) any judgment about the number of children to be made personally by the spouses themselves.

(II) The question is whether frequent copulation in marriage is necessary, even obligatory, to bring about and maintain the maximum values of the couple, the children and the family—not out of any egoistic hedonism, nor from a lack of moral generosity or continence, but from an incompatability between their duty and need of expressing conjugal love and at the same time of avoiding children in that very expression. The existence of sterile days does not afford a sufficient solution for modern society—because of the conditions of life, biological anomalies, psychological disturbances, the repression of spontaneity, the dangers to fidelity, etc. Recourse must be had to artificial ways of frustrating the natural generative power, by limiting its specific natural power, even if, normally and deliberately, it is ordered to the species and granted in marriage for the species. Therefore the use of contraceptives in marriage for the purpose of regulating children is presumed to be moral because it is specified by an honest intention, harmonizes the psychosomatic relationships between the spouses, is beneficial for their moral life and is of service to the procreative society. Some think it is evil, because it detracts something from the powers of nature, but it is a lesser evil, to be accepted humbly by fallen man rising with difficulty towards perfection. Others think it simply is good, indeed the optimum existential good possible for the present, fully legitimate because of the values and complex intention indicated above.

(6) *The concrete application to contraception* is made in this manner. Considered in itself contraception does not attain the ideal fullness of values. But it is not intrinsically evil. (Intrinsic evils are denied to creatures in man's horizontal plane.) In the concrete it is commonly licit and obligatory in marriage where the necessity of regulating children exists. No means and methods of obtaining this regulation are *a priori* immoral. In practice those are to be preferred which here and now better respect the complex finality of the action in humanitarian and existential values (the expression of love, the service to the procreative society, the more

198 NATIONAL CATHOLIC REPORTER

secure exclusion of undesired children, the intimacy and spontaneity of carnal gestures, the liberation of one's self or one's spouse's from distress, tension, etc.)

(7) The *principal arguments to legitimize contraception*. These vary from one to another whenever something new is proposed.

(a) In order *to supersede the traditional teaching,* they say that the traditional teaching, from an ignorance of biology, supposed that each individual conjugal act was by its nature ordained to children, and therefore erroneously thought that the order of nature was violated through use of an artificial means. They argue that Piux XI would not condemn such resort to artifice except when used for an arbitrary, egotistic-hedonistic reason vitiating the acts of nature; not when used for legitimate motives of expressing conjugal love in union, which contemporary investigations reveal prevails. They argue that this same Pontiff was not dealing with individual actions destined to the service of biological life of a future offspring but with the whole complex of conjugal life. About this, what he said is most rightly affirmed. They argue that the traditional teaching concerning contraception, since it was never defined (and cannot be defined because it is not in revelation), must be reformed, once the falsity has been demonstrated of its foundation with regard to children, as to the primary end of marriage (one out of every two hundred acts can be said to be generative) and with regard to false interpretation of Genesis 38: 8–10, and once its pessimism, stemming from an ignorance or a poor interpretation of sexual values, has been overcome.

(b) *On the level of experience,* they argue that, by

the testimony of the best doctors and married couples in modern life, periodic continence has been demonstrated to be impossible in itself, uncertain of biological regulation, harmful for the psychological life of the spouses, dangerous for conjugal fidelity and for the efficient regulation of offspring.

(c) *In the order of arguments from reason,* some insist on a dispensation from the principle of the lesser evil which often permits man in his fallen condition not only to consider but even to choose the lesser evil, even without physical necessity but with great moral fittingness. Others reject this prior consideration as injurious to the generosity of many couples and speak rather of the perplexity which persuades many to save the greater conjugal-family good, by sacrificing the lesser good of the physiological integrity of the act, as often and as easily as this can be repeated. Others, more generally, apply the principle of totality which permits the renunciation even of members and functions of organic life *(a fortiori,* therefore of their particular acts), not only for the health of the body or its functions, but even for the greater good of the person, both in the physical order and in the psychic order (cf. lobotomy). It follows that in conjugal life, through the physical evil of contraception, a psychic good may be obtained—the good of eliminating anxiety over a dangerous maternity, various obsessions, the inhibition of spontaneous love, etc. Some think that this principle probably applies also to the quasi-personal husband-wife union, so that the husband for the good of the wife, may impede the natural generative power of free genital action—for example, if she might conceive when she is weak or sick. And vice-versa, the wife may do so, lest her husband suffer tension by reason of conjugal continence, etc.

B. A Critique of This Position

(I) The *notion of the natural law* remains uncertain, changeable, withdrawn from the magisterium. For some, it may never be revealed; for others, only for a very special reason, in the rarest of cases, it proposes some relationship of man to God or to other men in acceptable arguments as definitive. (It is asserted that this never happened in history, certainly not in the solemn declaration of *Casti Connubii.*) This view does not do justice or protect either the competence which the Church has so many times vindicated for herself for the interpretation of the natural law, nor the Church's effective capacity of discerning the moral order established by God, which is so often obscure to fallen man.

(2) *Nature* seems to be understood as a complex of physical and psychic powers in the world, granted to the dominion of man, so that he can experience them, foster change, or frustrate them for his own earthly convenience. Numbered among these are the organs, powers, acts of man himself, without excepting such "super-personal" functions as the specifically genital actions ordered to the species. All these things, and in particular man's own psycho-physical parts, are conceived of as having been entrusted to the "embodied spirit" which is man, so that he may humanize them through his culture in a given set of physical possibilities. Therefore he can frustrate his own biological, sexual function, even, when voluntarily aroused, because it is subject to reason for the bettering of the human condition. Such earthly, cultural naturalism and utilitarian, exceedingly humanistic altruism, seem to allow insufficient place in human life for the action of the Holy Spirit and for his mission of healing sin. Neither is it evident what are the great demands on virtue which are often affirmed in this new tendency.

(3) Many things seem to be mixed up and confused when there is affirmed the mutability of nature in the human person according to the evolution of history. The essential distinction between mutations which are dependent on extrinsic conditions and the stability of principles deduced by right reason is ignored. Changes which are dependent on extrinsic conditions may permit or require contradictory moral actions in diverse situations, though under the same moral principle. One may cite, for example, heart surgery, which is now licit, but which once amounted to homicide. But the principles of right reason are deduced from a consideration of the essential relations of human nature, which constitute the norm of morality. For example, the different and complementary genitality of the sexes determines the right use of the generative function in Adam and Eve as in Titus and Sempronia. Many of the alleged changes in human nature are brought out by false reasoning and false interpretations of history, we can show; for example, that slavery became intrinsically evil or usury was permitted.

(4) The *authenticity of the magisterium* seems to be substantially violated:

(a) by *restricting its mission and power* beyond the limits vindicated by the Church for herself through the actions of several Pontiffs and through the First and Second Vatican Councils; and by reducing her competence so that she is deprived of her necessary authority to remain a light to the nations, teaching effectively the moral order established by God even when this is not clearly shown in Sacred Scripture and in apostolic tradition. Such is now claimed about onanism. Why should their contemporary solution be admitted any more than the statements of Pius XI or XII?

(b) by *confusing the consensus of the faithful* (of the Universal Church), of all who profess the common faith existing in all people of God, with the belief of the faithful (*Ecclesia discens,* the Church learning) which works together to illumine the hierarchy (*Ecclesia docens,* the Church teaching) in the quest for religious truths and in judging obscure and uncertain matters.

(c) by *taking away from the magisterium the authority* to discern the requirements of the natural law and to teach authoritatively when a large part of the faithful are in doubt. In this they approach the mentality of other Christian churches and offend against the genuine hierarchical constitution of the Church of Christ.

(d) by *not recognizing the differences* among the assents (to be given to truth) other than the difference between the infallible faith concerning things which have been revealed, and the assent of prudence concerning declarations reformable according to the developments of time, as is often the case in social matters. Thereby they ignore Catholic doctrines in the area of human actions which are plainly certain and morally irreformable, not to speak of theological conclusions constantly proved valid and of those things which some call "ecclesiastical faith." If contraception were declared not intrinsically evil, in honesty it would have to be acknowledged that the Holy Spirit in 1930, in 1951 and 1958, assisted Protestant churches, and that for half a century Pius XI, Pius XII and a great part of the Catholic hierarchy did not protect against a very serious error, one most pernicious to souls; for it would thus be suggested that they condemned most imprudently, under the pain of eternal punishment, thousands upon thousands of human acts which are now approved. Indeed, it must be neither denied nor ignored that these acts would be approved for the same fundamental reasons which Protestantism alleged and which they (Catholics) condemned or at least did not recognize. Therefore one must very cautiously inquire whether the change which is proposed would not bring along with it a definitive depreciation of the teaching and the moral direction of the hierarchy of the Church and whether several very grave doubts would not be opened up about the very history of Christianity.

(5) As for the *reasoning used* to justify contraception, among other things it seems: (a) To lack the fundamental distinction between the sexual condition of man and the free and voluntary use of the genital faculty. This latter is a particular aspect of man's sexual condition, about which in marriage a determined right is obtained. In theological tradition, this right is limited according to the natural ends of the generative faculties.

(b) If the specific use of this faculty can be turned aside in marriage from the generative finality, in the service of either the individual spouses, or of the family itself, or of a consort, why not outside of marriage? More of this later.

(c) Biology is said to have revealed both the falsity

of the ordering of each and every cojugal act toward generation, and the constant natural unitive quality of this act (which from the very beginning has been clear enough!), so that one might conclude that it is licit to contradict the generative power in order to satisfy the unitive tendency.

But (I) this conclusion is not at all apparent. For if an act is rarely generative, then one must exert care that it might produce its effect, while the expression of union which is constantly present could be more easily omitted in particular cases (for example, to procure fecundation artificially if it could not otherwise be obtained). There is a confusion between *inchoate procreativity,* which man actuates through a deliberative act, and *effective procreation,* which depends upon nature and has been removed from human deliberation by the Creator.

(II) There can be no contradiction between what Catholic teaching wished to signify through the term 'procreation-education' and which from the 16th century was commonly designated as a primary end of marriage, and the biology and physiology of the sexual act freely exercised. Any other finality, legitimately determining its use, must observe that integrity.

(III) Finally, it is not apparent how a freely placed act can be perfective of human nature, but at the same time be voluntarily mutilated and changed in its natural power, even if that frustration be for another good end. Indeed, that good can be obtained in another way—this is something which the contraceptive theory is always silent about—for conjugal love is above all spiritual (if the love is genuine) and it requires no specific carnal gesture, much less its repetition in some determined frequency. Consequently, the affirmed sense of generosity and the absence of hedonism are suspect, when we find the intimate love of the whole person between a father and daughter, a brother and sister, without the necessity of carnal gestures.

One final question might be asked: are not these men essentially limited by the influence of their time and culture and region and by organized propaganda so that they bring to the problem only a partial, transitory and vitiated vision, one that even now is not a fair response to the mind of very many people?

CONSEQUENCES IF THE TEACHING OF THE CHURCH IS CHANGED

A. As It Would Pertain to Moral Teaching in Sexual Matters

The great majority of theologians who argue that contraception is not absolutely illicit in individual conjugal acts posit the *principle of totality* as the basis for this opinion. This means that every partial good must be ordered to the good of the whole, and in a case of a conflict of interest a partial good must be sacrificed for the good of the whole. However, this principle is applied to the case differently by different people.

(1) A great number seem to admit that each and every sexual act is ordered by nature and ought to be ordered by man to procreation in its total complexity, i.e., understood as to include education. But education, in order that this might take place in a human way, requires a harmonious and balanced way of life by the parents and the whole family. This, in turn, requires

an undisturbed and spontaneous sexual life between the spouses. Therefore, individual conjugal acts ought to be ordered to this whole complex. A partial good, namely, the ordering of individual acts to procreation, can be sacrificed for the good of the whole, even if this does positively remove their procreative force.

Traditional teaching obviously admits the principle of totality and demands that the sexual act not take place except in relation to the whole reality of procreation and education. However, it maintains that each and every conjugal act of its very nature has a certain *specific, intrinsic, proper order,* inasmuch as by its nature it is both ordered to the whole reality of procreation, and in that way is ordered as an act of *bestowing life* (a creative action in the strict sense). To place an action which removes this specific ordination, intrinsically proper to it, even for the sake of a higher good, is to act contrary to the nature of things.

Once one has set aside this traditional principle, one would also be setting aside a *fundamental* criterion, up until the present time unshaken in its application to many acts which have always been considered by the Church to be serious sins against chastity.

(a) The *case of extra-marital sexual relationships* of those whose living together is ordered to the good of procreation understood as a total complex. So demanding might be those who are close to marriage but could not contract it at the moment because of difficulties, yet nevertheless feel bound to foster and make as secure as possible their future harmonious conjugal life together. Similarily demanding might be those who wish to test their mutual adaptability and their sexual compatibility for the good of the family. So also might be those in concubinage who neither can marry nor be separated from one another because of the children to be educated. This education also demands the harmonious home life of the parents and, of course, a peaceful sexual life.

It should be noted that these consequences are not imaginary, but actually are being defended by some Catholics in speech and in writing. It would seem that they are not illogical, once one abandons the principle of the specific ordering of each free, generative action to procreation in the strict sense.

(b) The *case of sexual acts in marriage,* for example, oral and anal copulation. They object that such acts as these will remain evil because they do not observe the intrinsic ordination of the conjugal act to a loving union. It could be answered, first of all, that it is not apparent why an ordination to procreation in the strict sense would not be required in every act, but nevertheless there would be required an ordination to loving union, as a good never to be sacrificed in single acts for the good of the whole. Then too, it stands to reason that some spouses experience the above described forms of intercourse as true amorous union. Nor is it apparent in this opinion why a loving union must be realized uniquely though the sexual organs of each. The same ought to be applied to mutual masturbation between the spouses, at least in the case where they cannot have intercourse. Or to the solitary masturbation of one spouse in the absence of the other, yet done with a certain marital affection, or as a means of releasing nervous pressure because of a long imposed

abstinence with possible damage to the peace and education of the family (for example in the case of the
illness of one spouse).

(c) Even further *the door is opened easily to the
licitness of masturbation* among youths on the ground
that it could be a remote preparation for realizing a
harmonious sexual life in marriage. Many psychologists
judge this to be a normal phase in adolescence for sound
sexual formation and maintain that its forced suppression could cause much wrong in such formation.

(d) *It is equally logical that direct sterilization would
be permitted* as well. For although sterilization in the
strict sense is commonly judged as a more serious intervention than the use of certain preventive means,
nevertheless several newer theologians (and it seems
quite logical) already admit the licitness even of this
kind of intervention for a contraceptive end, in the
case where the definitive removal of the fecundity of
conjugal acts through the use of merely contraceptive
media would not allow the couple to have sufficient
security and tranquility.

We admit that the illicity of several of the abuses
mentioned above is evident from Sacred Scriptures (as
also for several of those to be spoken of later). However, the exegetes generally agree that in those places
there is not being stated the positive law for Christians,
but simply the restatement of precepts of the natural
law. Therefore we return to the same question: on what
kind of basis does the prohibition of the natural law
rest? In other words, by the law set forth in Sacred
Scripture, is not a general prohibition for acting sexually
against the good of procreation included?

(2) However, many theologians, who maintain that

contraception is not intrinsically evil, seem to come to this conclusion from a more general principle: that, namely, which denies *all absolute intrinsic morality* to external human acts, in such a way that there is no human act which is so intrinsically evil that it cannot be justified because of a higher good of man. In stating this, they apply the principle that "the end specifies the means" and that "between two evils the lesser is to be chosen." They say that this specification and choice also include those things which are commonly called intrinsically evil.

If this principle is admitted, it would seem that more serious evils can yet be expected. Perhaps the promoters of the principle do not intend this. Nevertheless, these conclusions are actually drawn by others. Thus, for example, it could be concluded that masturbation is for the good of personal equilibrium, or homosexuality good for those who are affected with abnormal inclinations and seek only friendship with the same sex for their balance. The same could be done for the use of abortives or of abortion directly induced to save the life of the mother.

B. The Value and Dignity of the Church's Teaching Authority

If the Church should now admit that the teaching passed on is no longer of value, teaching which has been preached and stated with ever more insistent solemnity until very recent years, it must be feared greatly that its authority in almost all moral and dogmatic matters will be seriously harmed. For there are few moral truths so constantly, solemnly and, as it has appeared, definitively stated as this one for which it is now so quickly proposed that it be changed to the contrary.

What is more, however, this change would inflict a grave blow on the teaching about the assistance of the Holy Spirit promised to the Church to lead the faithful on the right way toward their salvation. For, as a matter of fact, the teaching of *Casti Connubii* was solemnly proposed in opposition to the doctrine of the Lambeth Conference of 1930, by the Church "to whom God has entrusted the defense of the integrity and purity of morals . . . in token of her divine ambassadorship . . . and through Our mouth." Is it nevertheless now to be admitted that the Church erred in this her work, and that the Holy Spirit rather assists the Anglican Church!

Some who fight for a change say that the teaching of the Church was not false for those times. Now, however, it must be changed because of changed historical conditions. But this seems to be something that one cannot propose, for the Anglican Church was teaching precisely that and for the very reasons which the Catholic Church solemnly denied, but which it would now admit. Certainly such a manner of speaking would be unintelligible to the people and would seem to be a specious pretext.

Others claim that the Church would be better off to admit her error, just as recently she has done in other circumstances. But this is no question of peripheral matters (as for example, the case of Galileo), or of an excess in the way a thing is done (the excommunication of Photius). This is a most significant question which profoundly enters into the practical lives of Christians in such a way that innumerable faithful would have been thrown by the magisterium into formal sin without material sin. But let there be consulted the serious words of Pius XI in his "Directive to priests who are confessors and who have the care of souls" (1930). Also let there be consulted the words of Pius XII in his "address to the cardinals and bishops on the occasion of the definition of the dogma of the Assumption of the Blessed Virgin Mary" (1950):

This way (namely, of liberation from the law of God) can never be taken because it is hurtful and harmful even when it is a question of someone who wishes to bring help to men in difficult situations of conjugal life. Therefore it would be pernicious to the Church and to civil society, if those who had care of souls, in teaching and in their way of life, would knowingly remain silent when the laws of God are violated in marriage. These laws always flourish, whatsoever the case may be.

For the Church to have erred so gravely in its grave responsibility of leading souls would be tantamount to seriously suggesting that the assistance of the Holy Spirit was lacking to her.

14

Humanae Vitae
"On Human Life"*

◆◆◆

Pope Paul VI

ENCYCLICAL ON THE REGULATION OF BIRTH

The following is a translation of the encyclical letter of Pope Paul VI, issued July 29, 1968, at the Vatican, on the regulation of birth.

Encyclical letter of His Holiness Pope Paul VI on the regulation of birth.

To the venerable Patriarchs, Archbishops and Bishops and other local ordinaries in peace and communion with the Apostolic See, to priests, the faithful and to all men of good will.

Venerable brothers and beloved sons:

* Translation by *NC News Service*.

The Transmission of Life

(1) The most serious duty of transmitting human life, for which married persons are the free and responsible collaborators of God the Creator, has always been a source of great joys to them, even if sometimes accompanied by not a few difficulties and by distress.

At all times the fulfillment of this duty has posed grave problems to the conscience of married persons, but, with the recent evolution of society, changes have taken place that give rise to new questions which the Church could not ignore, having to do with a matter which so closely touches upon the life and happiness of men.

I. NEW ASPECTS OF THE PROBLEM AND COMPETENCY OF THE MAGISTERIUM

New Formulation of the Problem

(2) The changes which have taken place are in fact noteworthy and of varied kinds. In the first place, there is the rapid demographic development. Fear is shown by many that world population is growing more rapidly than the available resources, with growing distress to many families and developing countries, so that the temptation for authorities to counter this danger with radical measures is great. Moreover, working and lodging conditions, as well as increased exigencies both in the economic field and in that of education, often make the proper education of an elevated number of children difficult today. A change is also seen both in the manner of considering the person of woman and her place in society, and in the value to be attributed to conjugal

love in marriage, and also in the appreciation to be made of the meaning of conjugal acts in relation to that love.

Finally and above all, man has made stupendous progress in the domination and rational organization of the forces of nature, such that he tends to extend this domination to his own total being: to the body, to psychical life, to social life and even to the laws which regulate the transmission of life.

(3) This new state of things gives rise to new questions. Granted the conditions of life today, and granted the meaning which conjugal relations have with respect to the harmony between husband and wife and to their mutual fidelity, would not a revision of the ethical norms, in force up to now, seem to be advisable, especially when it is considered that they cannot be observed without sacrifices, sometimes heroic sacrifices?

And again: by extending to this field the application of the so-called "principle of totality," could it not be admitted that the intention of a less abundant but more rationalized fecundity might transform a materially sterilizing intervention into a licit and wise control of birth? Could it not be admitted, that is, that the finality of procreation pertains to the ensemble of conjugal life, rather than to its single acts? It is also asked whether, in view of the increased sense of responsibility of modern man, the moment has not come for him to entrust to his reason and his will, rather than to the biological rhythms of his organism, the task of regulating birth.

Competency of the Magisterium

(4) Such questions required from the teaching authority of the Church a new and deeper reflection upon the principles of the moral teaching on marriage: a

teaching founded on the natural law, illuminated and enriched by divine revelation.

No believer will wish to deny that the teaching authority of the Church is competent to interpret even the natural moral law. It is, in fact, indisputable, as our predecessors have many times declared,[1] that Jesus Christ, when communicating to Peter and to the Apostles His divine authority and sending them to teach all nations His commandments,[2] constituted them as guardians and authentic interpreters of all the moral law, not only, that is, of the law of the gospel, but also of the natural law, which is also an expression of the will of God, the faithful fulfilment of which is equally necessary for salvation.[3]

Conformably to this mission of hers, the Church has always provided—and even more amply in recent times—a coherent teaching concerning both the nature of marriage and the correct use of conjugal rights and the duties of husband and wife.[4]

Special Studies

(5) The consciousness of that same mission induced us to confirm and enlarge the study commission which our predecessor Pope John XXIII of happy memory had instituted in March, 1963. That commission which included, besides several experts in the various pertinent disciplines also married couples, had as its scope the gathering of opinions on the new questions regarding conjugal life, and in particular on the regulation of births, and of furnishing opportune elements of information so that the magisterium could give an adequate reply to the expectation not only of the faithful, but also of world opinion.[5]

The work of these experts, as well as the successive

judgments and counsels spontaneously forwarded by or
expressly requested from a good number of our brothers
in the episcopate, have permitted us to measure more
exactly all the aspects of this complex matter. Hence
with all our heart we express to each of them our
lively gratitude.

Reply of the Magisterium

(6) The conclusions at which the commission arrived could not, nevertheless, be considered by us as
definitive, nor dispense us from a personal examination
of this serious question; and this also because, within
the commission itself, no full concordance of judgments
concerning the moral norms to be proposed had been
reached, and above all because certain criteria of solutions had emerged which departed from the moral
teaching on marriage proposed with constant firmness
by the teaching authority of the Church.

Therefore, having attentively sifted the documenta-
tion laid before us, after mature reflection and assiduous
prayers, we now intend, by virtue of the mandate entrusted to us by Christ, to give our reply to these grave
questions.

II. DOCTRINAL PRINCIPLES

A Total Vision of Man

(7) The problem of birth, like every other problem
regarding human life, is to be considered, beyond
partial perspectives—whether of the biological or psychological, demographic or sociological orders—in the
light of an integral vision of man and of his vocation,

not only his natural and earthly, but also his supernatural and eternal vocation. And since, in the attempt to justify artificial methods of birth control, many have appealed to the demands both of conjugal love and of "responsible parenthood" it is good to state very precisely the true concept of these two great realities of married life, referring principally to what was recently set forth in this regard, and in a highly authoritative form, by the Second Vatican Council in its pastoral constitution *Gaudium et Spes*.

Conjugal Love

(8) Conjugal love reveals its true nature and nobility when it is considered in its supreme origin, God, who is love,[6] "the Father, from whom every family in heaven and on earth is named".[7]

Marriage is not, then, the effect of chance or the product of evolution of unconscious natural forces; it is the wise institution of the Creator to realize in mankind His design of love. By means of the reciprocal personal gift of self, proper and exclusive to them, husband and wife tend towards the communion of their beings in view of mutual personal perfection, to collaborate with God in the generation and education of new lives.

For baptized persons, moreover, marriage invests the dignity of a sacramental sign of grace, inasmuch as it represents the union of Christ and of the Church.

Its Characteristics

(9) Under this light, there clearly appear the characteristic marks and demands of conjugal love, and it is of supreme importance to have an exact idea of these.

This love is first of all fully human, that is to say, of the senses and of the spirit at the same time. It is not, then, a simple transport of instinct and sentiment, but also, and principally, an act of the free will, intended to endure and to grow by means of the joys and sorrows of daily life, in such a way that husband and wife become one only heart and one only soul, and together attain their human perfection.

Then, this love is total, that is to say, it is a very special form of personal friendship, in which husband and wife generously share everything, without undue reservations or selfish calculations. Whoever truly loves his marriage partner loves not only for what he receives, but for the partner's self, rejoicing that he can enrich his partner with the gift of himself.

Again, this love is faithful and exclusive until death. Thus in fact do bride and groom conceive it to be on the day when they freely and in full awareness assume the duty of the marriage bond. A fidelity, this, which can sometimes be difficult, but is always possible, always noble and meritorious, as no one can deny. The example of so many married persons down through the centuries shows, not only that fidelity is according to the nature of marriage, but also that it is a source of profound and lasting happiness and finally, this love is fecund for it is not exhausted by the communion between husband and wife, but is destined to continue, raising up new lives. "Marriage and conjugal love are by their nature ordained toward the begetting and educating of children. Children are really the supreme gift of marriage and contribute very substantially to the welfare of their parents".[8]

Responsible Parenthood

(10) Hence conjugal love requires in husband and wife an awareness of their mission of "responsible parenthood," which today is rightly much insisted upon, and which also must be exactly understood. Consequently it is to be considered under different aspects which are legitimate and connected with one another.

In relation to the biological processes, responsible parenthood means the knowledge and respect of their functions; human intellect discovers in the power of giving life biological laws which are part of the human person.[9]

In relation to the tendencies of instinct or passion, responsible parenthood means that necessary dominion which reason and will must exercise over them.

In relation to physical, economic, psychological and social conditions, responsible parenthood is exercised, either by the deliberate and generous decision to raise a numerous family, or by the decision, made for grave motives and with due respect for the moral law, to avoid for the time being, or even for an indeterminate period, a new birth.

Responsible parenthood also and above all implies a more profound relationship to the objective moral order established by God, of which a right conscience is the faithful interpreter. The responsible exercise of parenthood implies, therefore, that husband and wife recognize fully their own duties towards God, towards themselves, towards the family and towards society, in a correct hierarchy of values.

In the task of transmitting life, therefore, they are not free to proceed completely at will, as if they could determine in a wholly autonomous way the honest path to follow; but they must conform their activity to the creative intention of God, expressed in the very nature of marriage and of its acts, and manifested by the constant teaching of the Church.[10]

Respect for the Nature and Purpose of the Marriage Act

(11) These acts, by which husband and wife are united in chaste intimacy, and by means of which human life is transmitted, are, as the council recalled, "noble and worthy",[11] and they do not cease to be lawful if, for causes independent of the will of husband and wife, they are foreseen to be infecund, since they always remain ordained towards expressing and consolidating their union. In fact, as experience bears witness, not every conjugal act is followed by a new life. God has wisely disposed natural laws and rhythms of fecundity which, of themselves, cause a separation in the succession of births. Nonetheless, the Church, calling men back to the observance of the norms of the natural law, as interpreted by their constant doctrine, teaches that each and every marriage act (*quilibet matrimonii usus*) must remain open to the transmission of life.[12]

Two Inseparable Aspects: Union and Procreation

(12) That teaching, often set forth by the magisterium, is founded upon the inseparable connection, willed by God and unable to be broken by man on his own initiative, between the two meanings of the conjugal act: the unitive meaning and the procreative

meaning. Indeed, by its intimate structure, the conjugal act, while most closely uniting husband and wife, capacitates them for the generation of new lives, according to laws inscribed in the very being of man and of woman. By safeguarding both these essential aspects, the unitive and the procreative, the conjugal act preserves in its fullness the sense of true mutual love and its ordination towards man's most high calling to parenthood. We believe that the men of our day are particularly capable of seizing the deeply reasonable and human character of this fundamental principle.

Faithfulness to God's Design

(13) It is in fact justly observed that a conjugal act imposed upon one's partner without regard for his or her condition and lawful desires is not a true act of love, and therefore denies an exigency of right moral order in the relationships between husband and wife. Hence, one who reflects well must also recognize that a reciprocal act of love, which jeopardizes the responsibility to transmit life which God the Creator, according to particular laws, inserted therein, is in contradiction with the design constitutive of marriage, and with the will of the Author of life. To use this divine gift destroying, even if only partially, its meaning and its purpose is to contradict the nature both of man and of woman and of their most intimate relationship, and therefore it is to contradict also the plan of God and His will. On the other hand, to make use of the gift of conjugal love while respecting the laws of the generative process means to acknowledge oneself not to be the arbiter of the sources of human life, but rather the

minister of the design established by the Creator. In fact, just as man does not have unlimited dominion over his body in general, so also, with particular reason, he has no such dominion over his generative faculties as such, because of their intrinsic ordination towards raising up life, of which God is the principle. "Human life is sacred," Pope John XXIII recalled, "from its very inception it reveals the creating hand of God".[13]

Illicit Ways of Regulating Birth

(14) In conforming with these landmarks in the human and Christian vision of marriage, we must once again declare that the direct interruption of the generative process already begun, and, above all, directly willed and procured abortion, even if for therapeutic reasons, are to be absolutely excluded as licit means of regulating birth.[14]

Equally to be excluded, as the teaching authority of the Church has frequently declared, is direct sterilization, whether perpetual or temporary, whether of the man or of the woman.[15] Similarly excluded is every action which, either in anticipation of the conjugal act, or in its accomplishment, or in the development of its natural consequences, proposes, whether as an end or as a means, to render procreation impossible.[16]

To justify conjugal acts made intentionally infecund, one cannot invoke as valid reasons the lesser evil, or the fact that such acts would constitute a whole together with the fecund acts already performed or to follow later, and hence would share in one and the same moral goodness. In truth, if it is sometimes licit to tolerate a lesser evil in order to avoid a greater evil or to promote a greater good [17] it is not licit, even for the gravest reasons, to do evil so that good may follow therefrom [18] that is, to make into the object of a positive act of the will something which is intrinsically disorder, and hence unworthy of the human person, even when the intention is to safeguard or promote individual, family or social well-being. Consequently it is an error to think that a conjugal act which is deliberately made infecund and so is intrinsically dishonest could be made honest and right by the ensemble of a fecund conjugal life.

Licitness of Therapeutic Means

(15) The Church, on the contrary, does not at all consider illicit the use of those therapeutic means truly necessary to cure diseases of the organism, even if an impediment to procreation, which may be foreseen, should result therefrom, provided such impediment is not, for whatever motive, directly willed.[19]

Licitness of Recourse to Infecund Periods

(16) To this teaching of the Church on conjugal morals, the objection is made today, as we observed earlier (no.3), that it is the prerogative of the human intellect to dominate the energies offered by irrational nature and to orientate them towards an end conformable to the good of man. Now, some may ask: In the present case, is it not reasonable in many circumstances to have recourse to artificial birth control if, thereby, we secure the harmony and peace of the family, and better conditions for the education of the

children already born? To this question it is necessary
to reply with clarity: the Church is the first to praise
and recommend the intervention of intelligence in a
function which so closely associates the rational creature with his Creator; but she affirms that this must be
done with respect for the order established by God.

If, then, there are serious motives to space out
births, which derive from the physical or psychological
conditions of husband and wife, or from external conditions, the Church teaches that it is then licit to take
into account the natural rhythms immanent in the generative functions, for the use of marriage in the infecund periods only, and in this way to regulate birth
without offending the moral principles which have been
recalled earlier.[20]

The Church is coherent with herself when she considers recourse to the infecund periods to be licit, while
at the same time condemning, as being always illicit,
the use of means directly contrary to fecundation, even
if such use is inspired by reasons which may appear
honest and serious. In reality, there are essential differences between the two cases; in the former, the
married couple make legitimate use of a natural dis-
position; in the latter, they impede the development of
natural processes. It is true that, in the one and the
other case, the married couple are concordant in the
positive will of avoiding children for plausible reasons,
seeking the certainty that offspring will not arrive; but
it is also true that only in the former case are they
able to renounce the use of marriage in the fecund
periods when, for just motives, procreation is not desirable, while making use of it during infecund periods
to manifest their affection and to safeguard their mutual

fidelity. By so doing, they give proof of a truly and integrally honest love.

Grave Consequences of Methods of Artificial Birth Control

(17) Upright men can even better convince themselves of the solid grounds on which the teaching of the Church in this field is based, if they care to reflect upon the consequences of methods of artificial birth control. Let them consider, first of all, how wide and easy a road would thus be opened up towards conjugal infidelity and the general lowering of morality. Not much experience is needed in order to know human weakness, and to understand that men—especially the young, who are so vulnerable on this point—have need of encouragement to be faithful to the moral law, so that they must not be offered some easy means of eluding its observance. It is also to be feared that the man, growing used to the employment of anti-conceptive practices, may finally lose respect for the woman and, no longer caring for her physical and psychological equilibrium, may come to the point of considering her as a mere instrument of selfish enjoyment, and no longer as his respected and beloved companion.

Let it be considered also that a dangerous weapon would thus be placed in the hands of those public authorities who take no heed of moral exigencies. Who could blame a government for applying to the solution of the problems of the community those means acknowledged to be licit for married couples in the solution of a family problem? Who will stop rulers from favoring, from even imposing upon their peoples, if they were to consider it necessary, the method of contraception which they judge to be most efficacious? In such a way men, wishing to avoid individual, family, or social difficulties encountered in the observance of the divine law, would reach the point of placing at the mercy of the intervention of public authorities the most personal and most reserved sector of conjugal intimacy.

Consequently, if the mission of generating life is not to be exposed to the arbitrary will of men, one must necessarily recognize unsurmountable limits to the possibility of man's domination over his own body and its functions; limits which no man, whether a private individual or one invested with authority, may licitly surpass. And such limits cannot be determined otherwise than by the respect due to the integrity of the human organism and its functions, according to the principles recalled earlier, and also according to the correct understanding of the "principle of totality" illustrated by our predecessor Pope Pius XII.[21]

The Church Guarantor of True Human Values

(18) It can be foreseen that this teaching will perhaps not be easily received by all: Too numerous are those voices—amplified by the modern means of propaganda—which are contrary to the voice of the Church. To tell the truth, the Church is not surprised to be made, like her divine founder, a "sign of contradiction",[22] yet she does not because of this cease to proclaim with humble firmness the entire moral law, both natural and evangelical. Of such laws the Church was not the author, nor consequently can she be their arbiter; she is only their depositary and their interpreter, without ever being able to declare to be licit that which

is not so by reason of its intimate and unchangeable opposition to the true good of man.

In defending conjugal morals in their integral wholeness, the Church knows that she contributes towards the establishment of a truly human civilization; she engages man not to abdicate from his own responsibility in order to rely on technical means; by that very fact she defends the dignity of man and wife. Faithful to both the teaching and the example of the Saviour, she shows herself to be the sincere and disinterested friend of men, whom she wishes to help, even during their earthly sojourn, "to share as sons in the life of the living God, the Father of all men".[23]

III. PASTORAL DIRECTIVES

The Church Mater et Magistra

(19) Our words would not be an adequate expression of the thought and solicitude of the Church, mother and teacher of all peoples, if, after having recalled men to the observance and respect of the divine law regarding matrimony, we did not strengthen them in the path of honest regulation of birth, even amid the difficult conditions which today afflict families and peoples. The Church, in fact, cannot have a different conduct towards men than that of the Redeemer: She knows their weaknesses, has compassion on the crowd, receives sinners; but she cannot renounce the teaching of the law which is, in reality, that law proper to a human life restored to its original truth and conducted by the spirit of God.[24] Though we are thinking also of

all men of good will, we now address ourself particularly to our sons, from whom we expect a prompter and more generous adherence.

Possibility of Observing the Divine Law

(20) The teaching of the Church on the regulation of birth, which promulgates the divine law, will easily appear to many to be difficult or even impossible of actuation. And indeed, like all great beneficent realities, it demands serious engagement and much effort, individual, family and social effort. More than that, it would not be practicable without the help of God, who upholds and strengthens the good will of men. Yet, to anyone who reflects well, it cannot but be clear that such efforts ennoble man and are beneficial to the human community.

Mastery of Self

(21) The honest practice of regulation of birth demands first of all that husband and wife acquire and possess solid convictions concerning the true values of life and of the family, and that they tend towards securing perfect self-mastery. To dominate instinct by means of one's reason and free will undoubtedly requires ascetical practices, so that the affective manifestations of conjugal life may observe the correct order, in particular with regard to the observance of periodic continence. Yet this discipline which is proper to the purity of married couples, far from harming conjugal love, rather confers on it a higher human value. It demands continual effort yet, thanks to its beneficent influence, husband and wife fully develop their per-

sonalities, being enriched with spiritual values. Such discipline bestows upon family life fruits of serenity and peace, and facilitates the solution of other problems; it favors attention for one's partner, helps both parties to drive out selfishness, the enemy of true love; and deepens their sense of responsibility. By its means, parents acquire the capacity of having a deeper and more efficacious influence in the education of their offspring; little children and youths grow up with a just appraisal of human values, and in the serene and harmonious development of their spiritual and sensitive faculties.

Creating an Atmosphere Favorable to Chastity

(22) On this occasion, we wish to draw the attention of educators, and of all who perform duties of responsibility in regard to the common good of human society, to the need of creating an atmosphere favorable to education in chastity, that is, to the triumph of healthy liberty over license by means of respect for the moral order.

Everything in the modern media of social communications which leads to sense excitation and unbridled customs, as well as every form of pornography and licentious performances, must arouse the frank and unanimous reaction of all those who are solicitous for the progress of civilization and the defense of the common good of the human spirit. Vainly would one seek to justify such depravation with the pretext of artistic or scientific exigencies,[25] or to deduce an argument from the freedom allowed in this sector by the public authorities.

Appeal to Public Authorities

(23) To rulers, who are those principally responsible for the common good, and who can do so much to safeguard moral customs, we say: Do not allow the morality of your peoples to be degraded; do not permit that by legal means practices contrary to the natural and divine law be introduced into that fundamental cell, the family. Quite other is the way in which public authorities can and must contribute to the solution of the demographic problem: namely, the way of a provident policy for the family, of a wise education of peoples in respect of moral law and the liberty of citizens.

We are well aware of the serious difficulties experienced by public authorities in this regard, especially in the developing countries. To their legitimate preoccupations we devoted our encyclical letter *Populorum Progressio*. But with our predecessor Pope John XXIII, we repeat: no solution to these difficulties is acceptable "which does violence to man's essential dignity" and is based only on an utterly materialistic conception of man himself and of his life. The only possible solution to this question is one which envisages the social and economic progress both of individuals and of the whole of human society, and which respects and promotes of true human values.[26] Neither can one, without grave injustice, consider divine providence to be responsible for what depends, instead, on a lack of wisdom in government, on an insufficient sense of social justice, on selfish monopolization, or again on blameworthy indolence in confronting the efforts and the sacrifices necessary to ensure the raising of living standards of a people and of all its sons.[27]

May all responsible public authorities—as some are already doing so laudably—generously revive their efforts. And may mutual aid between all the members of the great human family never cease to grow: This is an almost limitless field which thus opens up to the activity of the great international organizations.

To Men of Science

(24) We wish now to express our encouragement to men of science, who "can considerably advance the welfare of marriage and the family, along with peace of conscience, if by pooling their efforts they labor to explain more thoroughly the various conditions favoring a proper regulation of births".[28] It is particularly desirable that, according to the wish already expressed by Pope Pius XII, medical science succeed in providing a sufficiently secure basis for a regulation of birth, founded on the observance of natural rhythms.[29] In this way, scientists and especially Catholic scientists will contribute to demonstrate in actual fact that, as the Church teaches, "a true contradiction cannot exist between the divine laws pertaining to the transmission of life and those pertaining to the fostering of authentic conjugal love".[30]

To Christian Husbands and Wives

(25) And now our words more directly address our own children, particularly those whom God calls to serve Him in marriage. The Church, while teaching imperceptible demands of the divine law, announces the tidings of salvation, and by means of the sacraments opens up the paths of grace, which makes man a new

creature, capable of corresponding with love and true freedom to the design of his Creator and Saviour, and of finding the yoke of Christ to be sweet.[31]

Christian married couples, then, docile to her voice, must remember that their Christian vocation, which began at baptism, is further specified and reinforced by the sacrament of matrimony. By it husband and wife are strengthened and as it were consecrated for the faithful accomplishment of their proper duties, for the carrying out of their proper vocation even to perfection, and the Christian witness which is proper to them before the whole world.[32] To them the Lord entrusts the task of making visible to men the holiness and sweetness of the law which unites the mutual love of husband and wife with their cooperation with the love of God the author of human life.

We do not at all intend to hide the sometimes serious difficulties inherent in the life of Christian married persons; for them as for everyone else, "the gate is narrow and the way is hard, that leads to life".[33] But the hope of that life must illuminate their way, as with courage they strive to live with wisdom, justice and piety in this present time,[34] knowing that the figure of this world passes away.[35]

Let married couples, then, face up to the efforts needed, supported by the faith and hope which "do not disappoint . . . because God's love has been poured into our hearts through the Holy Spirit, who has been given to us".[36] Let them implore divine assistance by persevering prayer; above all, let them draw from the source of grace and charity in the eucharist. And if sin should still keep its hold over them, let them not be discouraged, but rather have recourse with humble perseverance to the mercy of God, which is poured forth in the sacrament of penance. In this way they will be enabled to achieve the fullness of conjugal life described by the Apostle: "husbands, love your wives, as Christ loved the Church . . . husbands should love their wives as their own bodies. He who loves his wife loves himself. For no man ever hates his own flesh, but nourishes and cherishes it, as Christ does the Church . . . this is a great mystery, and I mean in reference to Christ and the Church. However, let each one of you love his wife as himself, and let the wife see that she respects her husband".[37]

Apostolate in Homes

(26) Among the fruits which ripen forth from a generous effort of fidelity to the divine law, one of the most precious is that married couples themselves not infrequently feel the desire to communicate their experience to others. Thus there comes to be included in the vast pattern of the vocation of the laity a new and most noteworthy form of the apostolate of like to like; it is married couples themselves who become apostles and guides to other married couples. This is assuredly, among so many forms of apostolate, one of those which seem most opportune today.[38]

To Doctors and Medical Personnel

(27) We hold those physicians and medical personnell in the highest esteem who, in the exercise of their profession, value above every human interest the superior demands of their Christian vocation. Let them

persevere, therefore, in promoting on every occasion the discovery of solutions inspired by faith and right reason, let them strive to arouse this conviction and this respect in their associates. Let them also consider as their proper professional duty the task of acquiring all the knowledge needed in this delicate sector, so as to be able to give to those married persons who consult them wise counsel and healthy direction, such as they have a right to expect.

To Priests

(28) Beloved priest sons, by vocation you are the counselors and spiritual guides of individual persons and of families. We now turn to you with confidence. Your first task—especially in the case of those who teach moral theology—is to expound the Church's teaching on marriage without ambiguity. Be the first to give, in the exercise of your ministry, the example of loyal internal and external obedience to the teaching authority of the Church. That obedience, as you know well, obliges not only because of the reasons adduced, but rather because of the light of the Holy Spirit, which is given in a particular way to the pastors of the Church in order that they may illustrate the truth [39]. You know, too, that it is of the utmost importance, for peace of consciences and for the unity of the Christian people, that in the field of morals as well as in that of dogma, all should attend to the magisterium of the Church, and all should speak the same language. Hence, with all our heart we renew to you the heartfelt plea of the great Apostle Paul: "I appeal to you, brethren, by the name of Our Lord Jesus Christ, that all of you

agree and that there be no dissensions among you, but that you be united in the same mind and the same judgment" [40].

(29) To diminish in no way the saving teaching of Christ constitutes an eminent form of charity for souls. But this must ever be accompanied by patience and goodness, such as the Lord himself gave example of in dealing with men. Having come not to condemn but to save [41], he was indeed intransigent with evil, but merciful towards individuals.

In their difficulties, may married couples always find, in the words and in the heart of a priest, the echo of the voice and the love of the Redeemer.

To Bishops

(30) Beloved and venerable brothers in the episcopate, with whom we most intimately share the solicitude of the spiritual good of the people of God, at the conclusion of this encyclical our reverent and affectionate thoughts turn to you. To all of you we extend an urgent invitation. At the head of the priests, your collaborators, and of your faithful, work ardently and incessantly for the safeguarding and the holiness of marriage, so that it may always be lived in its entire human and Christian fullness. Consider this mission as one of your most urgent responsibilities at the present time. As you know, it implies concerted pastoral action in all the fields of human activity, economic, cultural and social; for, in fact, only a simultaneous improvement in these various sectors will make it possible to render the life of parents and of children within their families not only tolerable, but easier and more joyous, to render the

living together in human society more fraternal and
peaceful, in faithfulness to God's design for the world.

Final Appeal

(31) Venerable brothers, most beloved sons, and all
men of good will, great indeed is the work of education, of progress and of love to which we call you,
upon the foundation of the Church's teaching, of which
the successor of Peter is, together with his brothers in
the episcopate, the depositary and interpreter. Truly a
great work, as we are deeply convinced, both for the
world and for the Church, since man cannot find true
happiness—towards which he aspires with all his being
—other than in respect of the laws written by God in
his very nature, laws which he must observe with intelligence and love. Upon this work, and upon all of
you, and especially upon married couples, we invoke
the abundant graces of the God of holiness and mercy,
and in pledge thereof we impart to you all our apostolic
blessing.

Given at Rome, from St. Peter's, this 25th day of
July, feast of St. James the Apostle, in the year 1968,
the sixth of our pontificate.

PAULUS PP.VI.

NOTES

1. Cf. Pius IX, encyclical *Qui Pluribus*, Nov. 9, 1846; in *PII
IX P. M. Acta*, I, pp. 9-10; St. Pius X, encyc. *Singulari Quadam*,
Sept. 24, 1912; in *AAS IV* (1912), p. 658; Pius XI, encyc. *Casti
Connubii*, Dec. 31, 1930; in *AAS* XXII (1930), pp. 579–581; Pius
XII, allocution *Magnificate Dominum* to the episcopate of the
Catholic world, Nov. 2, 1954; in *AAS* XLVI (1954), pp. 671–672; John
XXIII, encyc. *Mater et Magistra*, May 15, 1961; in *AAS* LIII (1961),
p. 457.

2. Cf. Matt. 28, 18–19.

3. Cf. Matt, 7, 21.

4. Cf. *Catechismus Romanus Concilii Tridentini*, part II, ch. VIII; Leo XIII, encyc. *Arcanum*, Feb. 19, 1880; in *Acta Leonis* XIII, II (1881), pp. 26–29; Pius XI, encyc. *Divini Illius Magistri*, Dec. 31, 1929, in *AAS* XXII (1930), pp. 58–61; encyc. *Casti Connubii*, in *AAS* XXII (1930), pp. 545–546; Pius XII, alloc. to the Italian medicobiological union of St. Luke, Nov. 12, 1944, in *Discorsi e Radiomessaggi*, VI, pp. 191–192; to the Italian Catholic union of midwives Oct. 29, 1951, in *AAS* XLIII (1951), pp. 857–859; to the seventh Congress of the International Society of Haematology, Sept. 12, 1958, in *AAS* L (1958), pp. 734–735; John XXIII, encyc. *Mater et Magistra*, in *AAS* LIII (1961), pp. 446–447; *Codex Iuris Canonici*, Canon 1067; Can. 1968, S 1, Can. 1066 S 1–2; Second Vatican Council, Pastoral Constitution *Gaudium et Spes*, nos. 47–52.

5. Cf. Paul VI, allocution to the Secred College, June 23, 1964, in *AAS* LVI (1964), p. 558; to the Commission for Study of Problems of Population, Family and Birth, March 27, 1965, in *AAS* LVII (1965), p. 388, to the National Congress of the Italian Society of Obstetrics and Gynaecology, Oct. 29, 1966, in *AAS* LVIII (1966), p. 1168.

6. Cf. I John, 4, 8.

7. Cf. Eph., 3, 15.

8. Cf. II Vat. Council, Pastoral const. *Gaudium et Spes*, No. 50.

9. Cf. St. Thomas, *Summa Theologica*, I–II, q. 94, art. 2.

10. Cf. Pastoral Const. *Gaudium et Spes*, nos. 50, 51.

11. *Ibid.*, no. 49.

12. Cf. Pius XI, encyc. *Casti Connubii*, in *AAS* XXII (1930), p. 560; Pius XII, in *AAS* XLIII (1951), p. 843.

13. Cf. John XXIII, encyc. *Mater et Magistra*, in *AAS* LIII (1961), p. 447.

14. Cf. *Catechismus Romanus Concilii Tridentini*, part. II, Ch. VIII; Pius XI, encyc. *Casti Connubii*, in *AAS* XXII (1930), pp. 562–564; Pius XII, *Discorsi e Radiomessaggi*, VI (1944), pp. 191–192; *AAS* XLIII (1951), pp. 842–843; pp. 857–859; John XXIII, encyc. *Pacem in Terris*, April 11, 1963, in *AAS* LV (1963), pp. 259–260; *Gaudium et Spes*, no. 51.

15. Cf. Pius XI, encyc. *Casti Connubii*, in *AAS* XXII (1930) p. 565; decree of the Holy Office, Feb. 22, 1940, in *AAS* L (1958), pp. 734–735.

16. Cf. *Catechismus Romanus Concilii Tridentini*, part. II, Ch. VIII; Pius XI, encyc. *Casti Connubii*, in *AAS* XXII (1930), pp. 559–561; Pius XII, *AAS* XLIII (1951), p. 843; *AAS* L. (1958), pp. 734–735; John XXIII, encyc. *Mater et Magistra*, in *AAS* LIII (1961) p. 447.

17. Cf. Pius XII, alloc. to the National Congress of the Union of Catholic Jurists, Dec. 6, 1953, in *AAS* XLV (1953), pp. 798–799.

18. Cf. Rom. 3, 8.

19. Cf. Pius XII, alloc. to Congress of the Italian Association of Urology, Oct. 8, 1953, in *AAS* XLV (1953), pp. 674–675; *AAS* L (1958) pp. 734–735.

20. Cf. Pius XII, *AAS* XLIII (1951), p. 846.

21. Cf. *AAS* XLV (1953), pp. 674–675; *AAS* XLVIII (1956), pp. 461–462.

22. Cf. Luke 2, 34.

23. Cf. Paul VI, encyc. *Populorum Progressio*, March 26, 1967, No. 21.

24. Cf. Rom. 8.

25. Cf. II Vatican Council, decree *Inter Mirifica on the Media of Social Communication*, nos. 6–7.

26. Cf. encyc. *Mater et Magistra*, in *AAS* LIII (1961), p. 447.

27. Cf. encyc. *Populorum Progressio*, Nos. 48–55.

28. Cf. Pastoral Const. *Gaudium et Spes*, No. 52.

29. Cf. *AAS* XLIII (1951), p. 859.

30. Cf. Pastoral Const. *Gaudium et Spes*, No. 51.

31. Cf. Matt. 11, 30.

32. Cf. Pastoral Const. *Gaudium et Spes*, No. 48, II Vatican Council, Dogmatic Const. *Lumen Gentium*, No. 35.

33. Matt. 7, 14; cf. Heb. 11, 12.

34. Cf. Tit. 2, 12.

35. Cf. I Cor.: 7, 31.

36. Cf. Rom. 5, 5.

37. Eph. 5, 25, 28–29, 32–33.

38. Cf. Dogmatic Const. *Lumen Gentium*, Nos. 35 and 41; Pastoral Const. *Gaudium et Spes*, Nos. 48–49; II Vatican Council, Decree *Apostolicam Actuositatem*, No. 11.

39. Cf. Dogmatic Const. *Lumen Gentium*, No. 25.

40. Cf. I Cor.: 1, 10.

41. Cf. John 3, 17.

Contributors

FATHER GREGORY BAUM is professor of theology at St. Michael's College in the University of Toronto and director of the Center for Ecumenical Studies. He is the author, most recently, of *The Credibility of the Church Today* (Herder and Herder).

SIDNEY CALLAHAN, the mother of six children, is the author of *The Illusion of Eve* and *Beyond Birth Control* (both Sheed and Ward). At present she is doing graduate work in psychology at Sarah Lawrence.

FATHER CHARLES E. CURRAN is professor of moral theology at the Catholic University of America. He is the author of *Christian Morality Today* (Fides) and the editor of *Absolutes in Moral Theology?* (Corpus Books).

DR. THOMAS F. DRAPER, the father of seven children, is director of public health in Newtown, Conn., and a practicing pediatrician.

FATHER BERNARD HÄRING, C.SS.R., is professor of moral theology at the Alphonsian Institute in Rome. Among his numerous books is *The Law of Christ* (three volumes, Newman Press).

JOHN T. NOONAN, JR., is professor of law at the University of California, Berkeley. A member of the Papal Birth Control Commission he was also author of *Contraception* (Harvard University Press, 1965).

MICHAEL NOVAK is chairman of the Humanities Department at the State University of New York at Old Westbury. He has taught at Stanford University and among his numerous books is *Belief and Unbelief* (Macmillan).

JULIAN PLEASANTS is a research biologist at the Lobund Laboratory at the University of Notre Dame. He was a contributor to *Contraception and Holiness* (Herder and Herder).

MARY PERKINS RYAN and JOHN JULIAN RYAN, the parents of five sons, are the coauthors of *Love and Sexuality: A Christian Approach* (Holt, Rinehart and Winston).

The Editor:

DANIEL CALLAHAN is the author of *The Mind of the Catholic Layman, Honesty in the Church* and *The New Church*. He is also editor of *The Secular City Debate* and *Generation of the Third Eye* and has contributed to many periodicals. Dr. Callahan, a graduate of Yale University, received his M.A. from Georgetown University and a Ph.D. in philosophy from Harvard. He was formerly executive editor of *Commonweal*. At present, he is completing a book on abortion under a grant from The Population Council and The Food Foundation.